KAYAK FISHING

THE ULTIMATE GUIDE

By Captain Scott Null and Joel McBride

For Svng
From Wally
Be Prepared

KAYAK FISHING
THE ULTIMATE GUIDE

By Captain Scott Null and Joel McBride

PHOTOS BY JOCK BRADLEY

Published by

 THE **HELICONIA PRESS**

1576 Beachburg Road
Beachburg, Ontario K0J 1C0
www.helipress.com

Printed in Singapore

First Edition

ISBN # 978-1-896980-28-7

Written by: Scott Null and Joel McBride
Photography by: Jock Bradley
Design and Layout: Vicki Veenstra
Edited by: Rebecca Sandiford

Library and Archives Canada Cataloguing in Publication

Null, Scott, 1963-
    Kayak fishing : the ultimate guide / by Scott Null and Joel
McBride ; editor: Rebecca Sandiford ; photographer: Jock Bradley.

ISBN 978-1-896980-28-7

1. Kayak fishing. 2. Saltwater fishing. I. Bradley, Jock, 1961-
II. Sandiford, Rebecca, 1973- III. McBride, Joel, 1966- IV. Title.

SH446.K39N84 2007   799.16   C2006-907023-7

ABOUT SAFETY

Kayaking, fishing, and kayak fishing are all activities with inherent risks, and this book is designed as a general guide, not a substitute for experience. The publisher and the authors do not take responsibility for the use of any of the materials or methods described in this book. By following any of the procedures described within, you do so at your own risk.

TABLE OF CONTENTS

ABOUT THE AUTHORS VIII
Captain Scott Null VIII
Joel McBride IX

PHOTOGRAPHY X

SPECIAL CONTRIBUTORS XI

INTRODUCTION XIII

FOREWORD XV

CHAPTER ONE: EQUIPMENT 17
Kayaks   18
   Sit-On-Top Kayaks (SOTS)   19
   Sit-Inside Kayaks (SINKS)   20
   Choosing a Kayak   21
   Paddles   22
   Paddle Leashes   24
PFDs (Personal Flotation Devices)   24
Accessories   25
   Seats   25
   Rod Holders   25
   Paddle Holders   28
   Anchors   28
   Stowage   31
   Fish Finders and Depth Sounders   32
   Thigh Straps   32
   Spray Skirts   32
   Rudders   33
   Installing Accessories   33
Clothing   35
   Dressing for Warm Water Conditions   35
   Dressing for Cold Water Conditions   35
Safety Gear   38
   Water and Energy Bars   38
   First Aid Kit   38
   Emergency Bag   38

   Spare Paddle   38
   Paddle Floats   38
   Bilge Pumps   39
   Communication Devices   39
   Signaling Devices   40
   Navigation Tools   40

CHAPTER 2: BEFORE HITTING THE WATER 43
Care and Maintenance for Your Kayak and Gear   44
Transporting Your Kayak   45
Carrying Your Kayak   46
Packing Your Kayak   47
Getting In and Out of Your Kayak   48
Sitting In a Kayak   50
Using Your Paddle   51
Using Rudders or Skegs   53
Choosing a Kayak Fishing Location   55
   Choosing a Good Launch   56

CHAPTER 3: THE ESSENTIAL STROKES AND SAFETY . . 58
Forward Stroke   60
   Catch   60
   Rotation   61
   Recovery   63
Reverse Stroke   63
   Using the Reverse Stroke as a Brake   63
Sweep Strokes   65
   Forward Sweep   65
   Reverse Sweep   65
Draw Strokes   68
   Basic Draw   68
   T-Stroke Draw   68
   Sculling Draw   70
Re-entering Your Kayak from the Water   71
   Re-entering a Sit-On-Top   72
   Re-entering a Sit-Inside   73

CHAPTER 4: FISHING FROM A KAYAK 77

Trolling	79
Drift Fishing	80
Side-Saddle Fishing	82
Poling	83
Wade Fishing from a Kayak	84
Fly Fishing	87
Using Bait	88
Using Lures	89
Fishing from a Tandem	91
Fishing with Kids	92
Using a Power Boat as a Mothership	93
On-the-Water Safety	95
Dealing with Weather	97

CHAPTER 5: CATCHING FISH 99

Fighting Fish from a Kayak	103
Landing Fish in a Kayak	105

CHAPTER 6: FRESHWATER KAYAK FISHING 111

Fishing Lakes and Ponds	113
Fishing Flowing Rivers	113
Classes of Rivers	113
Anatomy of a River	115
Getting to the Fish	116
From Put-In to Take-Out	116
River Hazards and Safety	116

CHAPTER 7: SALTWATER KAYAK FISHING 121

Understanding Tides and Tidal Currents	122
Dealing with Surf	124
Saltwater Fishing Hazards and Safety	124
Sharks	125
Stingrays	126
Other Creatures	127
Weather	127
Tides and Currents	128
The Other Guy	129

GLOSSARY OF TERMS 130

ABOUT THE AUTHORS

CAPTAIN SCOTT NULL

Captain Scott Null grew up fishing the waters of the Galveston Bay Complex, and has hunted and fished on the Texas coast his whole life. Spurred by his adventurous spirit and desire to explore new waters, he has fished all along the Gulf Coast from the southern tip of Texas to the Florida Everglades.

Scott spends most of his time in the marshes, bayous, and flats of the Upper Texas Coast, where he uses a kayak to stalk shallow foraging redfish. When he isn't fishing for himself he shares his love of the outdoors and extensive knowledge with others through his guiding company Let's Go Fishing.

Scott is a retired homicide detective who worked for the Houston Police Department for twenty-one years. He is currently the regional sales representative for Confluence Watersports, covering Texas, Oklahoma, and Louisiana. He writes a monthly column on kayak fishing for Gulf Coast Connections magazine and has authored several fishing articles for Paddler Magazine.

JOEL MCBRIDE

Joel McBride is a passionate and knowledgeable whitewater kayaker and fisherman, having frequently paddled and fished both rivers and freshwater lakes since he was a boy growing up in Maine. Now 39 years old, Joel lives along the banks of the Arkansas River with his wife and two daughters in the small mountain town of Salida, Colorado. He has worked in sales and marketing for the most prominent paddlesports manufacturers for the past 15 years and although his days are busy, he never misses an opportunity to get his feet wet.

PHOTOGRAPHY

JOCK BRADLEY

Whether bushwhacking through Philippine jungles, rappelling into vertical gorges or diving deep into the ocean, Jock consistently overcomes tremendous obstacles to obtain the perfect shot. It is, above all, this type of dedication and work ethic that sets him apart—making him one of the world's foremost professional outdoor photographers. For more info, visit www.jockbradley.com.

SPECIAL CONTRIBUTORS

CAPTAIN DEAN "SLOWRIDE" THOMAS

Dean and his wife Jennifer run Slowride Guide Service in Aransas Pass, Texas. Dean plies his trade in the Redfish Bay area which is one of the most popular kayak fishing destinations on the Texas coast. These shallow grass flats are home to a healthy population of speckled trout and redfish, and Dean knows the flats better than anyone. Whether you are looking for a fully guided fishing trip or just want to rent a kayak and go exploring on your own, the Thomas duo will take great care of you. Check out their website, www.slowrideguide.com.

CAPTAINS EVERETT (EJ) AND PAM JOHNSON

EJ and Pam are probably two of the busiest people in the Texas outdoors scene. Together they run Gulf Coast Connections Guide Service guiding anglers by power boat and kayaks to some of the most pristine marshes on the Texas coast located along the back side of Matagorda Island. Not only can EJ guide you to some awesome fishing, he can also provide you with a running narrative on the history and natural wonders of the area. On top of all this, EJ and Pam publish Texas Saltwater Fishing Magazine, the only publication dedicated solely to the Texas saltwater fishing enthusiast. For guided trips, contact EJ or Pam at 361-550-3637. For more information about the magazine, go to www.gulfcoastconnections.com.

CAPTAIN CHARLES (CHUCK) WRIGHT

Captain Wright owns and operates Chokoloskee Charters in the heart of the Everglades. From his home on the water he guides fishermen to the remote reaches of the last great frontier of fishing in the continental United States. When you climb aboard his twenty-eight foot mothership Yak Attack, you're beginning the adventure of a lifetime. Captain Chuck uses the boat to transport people and kayaks to areas of the Everglades that seldom see an angler, much less a kayak angler. Paddling deep into the Everglades is a truly special experience, and Chuck is the right guy to make it happen. To get in touch with Captain Wright go to www.chokoloskeecharters.com.

BRENDAN MARK

Growing up on the Ottawa River, Brendan has been both a dedicated paddler and angler since he was kid. Throughout his teens and early twenties, Brendan committed himself to his obsession with kayaking, and reached his ultimate paddling goal in 2003 by winning the World Championships in Austria. Shortly thereafter, having retired from competitive kayaking, Brendan realized that he could combine his two favorite activities—whitewater kayaking and fishing—and discovered that it allowed him to access huge stretches of water that have likely never seen lures. With an honors business degree in marketing, and a passion for the outdoors, Brendan is the marketing director for The Heliconia Press—publishers of this book.

INTRODUCTION

By Scott Null

Fishing from a kayak? Sounds crazy to those who have never heard of it or experienced it, but kayak fishing is currently one of the fastest growing sports in America. Even the most ardent wade angler and skiff angler is easily lured into kayak fishing by its ease of use and the access it provides to new waters.

I often get the question, "Why would you fish from a kayak when you've got a perfectly good boat?" I have a standard answer for this near-constant question: I use a kayak so that I can go where it's too shallow for boats and too muddy for wading. My home waters are the Galveston Bay Complex. You'd be hard pressed to find an area on the Texas coast with more fishing pressure than this bay system. The kayak has allowed me to explore and fish in places that are virtually inaccessible to power boats—and in the process I've managed to escape the crowds and find fish that rarely see a lure.

Even though this was the main reason I got into fishing from a kayak, I've come to learn that kayaks are great for all kinds of fishing. I can paddle out to the open bay and drift a reef or I can bust through the surf and fish the outer bar in relative comfort. They're also perfectly at home on a small stream or a big freshwater lake. I've even paddled several miles out into the Gulf of Mexico seeking bigger and meaner game fish. Modern kayaks are one of the most versatile and easy-to-use crafts available. There are all kinds of kayaks designed to fit a wide variety of people and fishing situations. Just match the kayak to the job and head out on your adventure.

A kayak fishing trip can be as simple or as complex as you want. A quick trip to a nearby waterway after work can be a perfect end to a stressful day. I've found that these trips can happen frequently because they don't take much pre-trip planning—and nor do they require much in the way of post-trip chores. I keep my basic kayak fishing gear stowed in the garage where it is easy to grab on a moment's notice. I drive to the shore, put the kayak in the water and go. It's truly amazing what a couple hours on the water can do for the psyche. When the trip is over, if I don't have time to clean the boat, it can wait until tomorrow or even the next day. I can even skip the late evening chore of unloading the kayak from the truck by simply locking it in place. There is some smug satisfaction to be had while driving through traffic the next morning with a kayak still strapped to the truck.

Contrast this scenario with a trip in my pre-kayak days. Does the boat have gas? How's the battery? Are the wheel bearings greased? Then it was time to hook up the boat and tow it to a ramp, pay the ramp fee, launch the boat, and park the truck before I even got around to thinking about any fishing. When the trip was over it was time to clean up the boat, flush the engine with fresh water, and drop it off at the storage shed. Over the years I had come to the point where quick trips after work just weren't worth the effort. A busy day at work followed by a hectic scramble to get in a couple hours of fishing was not exactly relaxing and therapeutic.

This book was born as an idea for prompting people with fishing skills who were on the fence about kayak fishing to go ahead and jump in. As the project progressed, we realized that many longtime kayakers were likely thinking about getting into it from the other direction, so we added some content for them. Now that it's done, I'm confident that this book offers new kayak anglers a solid foundation in skills and concepts that will allow a safe, comfortable entry into the sport. At the same time, experienced kayak anglers will learn how to get the most out of their time spent on the water. Ultimately, whether you're new to kayak fishing or already experienced, it is our hope that this book serves to make your experiences on the water safer, more productive, and most of all, more enjoyable.

FOREWORD

It is my privilege to write the foreword to Scott Null and Joel McBride's book *Kayak Fishing: An Essential Guide*. I know them both very well and can vouch for their character, their knowledge, their enthusiasm and their desire to help others experience and enjoy the unique world of kayak fishing. Scott is a lifelong coastal fisherman with nearly 30 years of experience here in Texas. The considerable knowledge he has gained as a recreational angler, tourney angler, charter captain and kayak fishing guide make him a perfect candidate to co-author a book like this. Joel grew up in Maine and has made his home in Colorado for the past 20 years. Joel has a great passion for whitewater paddling, and mountain stream and river angling. He also brings a wealth of valuable experience to the co-authoring of this book. Scott and Joel have been very influential in guiding the sport of kayak fishing during its infancy, and continue to do so now, when it is enjoying immense popularity in many parts of this country.

It wasn't very long ago that if you carried a kayak on your vehicle, or paddled onto the flats or into the salt marshes of Texas, pretty near everybody who saw you would scratch their head and ask whether you'd lost your marbles. Texas, you see, was the birthplace (and is still a stronghold) of shallow water skiffs that can traverse the flats and that seem able to glide on little more than dew. Serious shallow-water enthusiasts can be likened to cowboys in a way; neither could be considered fond of dismounting—especially if their next mode of transport required a paddle!

My personal paddle sport experiences span more decades than I like to admit, and so kayak fishing, when I got the chance, seemed a natural thing for me. It was introduced to me in the earlier days by several old salts who "mother-shipped" their plastic boats to the backcountry in vessels that drafted in feet, not the mere inches that redfish are very happy to thrive in. The game then was simple; when the fish were in the marsh, you'd run the big boat as close as you could, and then paddle in after them. The boats that were available to early kayak fishermen were hardly designed for the purpose, so we tried not to paddle any farther than necessary, and the stuff we equipped our boats with was almost comical—unless you were the guy trying to use it. In fact, many of us struggled through an assortment of pirogues, canoes, inflatables and various touring boats that we tried to adapt as fishing crafts before finally acquiring a modern sit-on-top kayak that was designed entirely for fishing.

We can thank Scott and Joel and others like them for their contributions to modern day design. The boats we have today are a joy to paddle and are designed to accept a dizzying array of accessories and accoutrements that make our fishing more fun and productive. When I think of some of the junk I've paddled and some of the crazy ideas my fishing buddies and I have tried, I am quick to say, "Read this book carefully and pay attention to what Scott and Joel have to say. You can become an expert kayak fisherman in a short time." The knowledge that you can acquire from reading this book will save you a lot of the grief the old-timers had to experience.

Today, we see kayak fishing really coming into its own. We have more people paddling right from the dock to the fishing grounds than we had back when mother shipping was considered the hot setup. Scott and Joel have put this book together in such a way that I believe there is important knowledge here for paddlers and anglers of all skill levels. The advice they give for rigging and equipping your boat and selecting your gear will be invaluable to beginners; and no matter how many times you've done it on your own, ideas, observations and recommendations from true experts are always worth your time and consideration. I hope that you will find this book as entertaining and informative as I have.

Wishing you all the best in fishing and paddling,

Everett Johnson

Editor and Publisher
Gulf Coast Connections – Texas Saltwater Fishing Magazine

Kayaks

Paddles

Accessories

Clothing

Safety Gear

EQUIPMENT

chapter one

1

KAYAKS

With the sport of kayak fishing growing at a steady rate, there are more than a few manufacturers producing kayaks intended specifically for kayak fishing. If you're just getting into the sport, then the number of different boat designs available can make choosing a kayak seem overwhelming. It doesn't have to be. By clearly identifying how and where you'll be using the kayak, you can quickly narrow down your options. In particular, it will let you decide which of the two self-explanatory styles you should be considering: a Sit-On-Top kayak (SOT) or a Sit-Inside kayak (SINK).

Both SOTs and SINKs are available as hard shell boats and as inflatables. Hard shells are generally more popular, because they require no set-up. Inflatable kayaks are an option that some might consider because they are much easier to transport when they've been deflated. However, there are some points to consider before choosing an inflatable. Keep in mind the type of terrain you'll be fishing. Are there sharp rocks, downed trees, or shallow oysters? How about the hooks you're using and sharp teeth of some fish? Unless it is your only option, we would suggest you steer away from inflatable kayaks for serious fishing because of the ever-present danger of a puncture that could compromise your safety.

Although SOTs and SINKs have some differences, they share many of the same parts. The top of a kayak is referred to as the deck. The bottom is the hull. The front of the boat is called the bow, the back is the stern, and most will have carrying handles at each end. Some kayaks also have rudders or skegs to assist you in tracking (going straight) or steering. SOTs and SINKs both have seats and some form of support for the feet. The better models tend to have built-in backrests, although some of the best backrests are bought separately from the kayak and then installed.

The differences between SOTs and SINKs are quite simple. With a SOT, your seating area is literally on the top deck of the kayak. With a SINK, you are sitting inside the craft in a cockpit. Around the cockpit of a SINK you'll find the cockpit rim, otherwise referred to as the coaming. This raised lip allows a skirt to be attached to the boat in order to keep water out or sun off the legs. SINKs have foot pedals inside which can be adjusted fore and aft to accommodate paddlers with different leg lengths. While many SOT kayaks also have foot pedals,

Sit-on-top kayak

Sit-inside kayak

some only have foot wells. Foot wells are a series of bumps that protrude from the kayak at measured intervals, in which you place your feet. Foot wells are nice and simple, but foot pedals provide the most support and are more comfortable to use, especially if you're spending a full day on the water. Foot pedals are also necessary to control the rudder if the kayak is equipped with one.

Now that we've looked at the main similarities and differences between SOTs and SINKs, let's look at their advantages and disadvantages.

SIT-ON-TOP KAYAKS (SOTS)

The sit-on-top is by far the most popular style of kayak for paddling anglers today and for good reason. The SOT leaves you free to move about, sit side-saddle, or step off to wade fish with ease. The SOT also alleviates the fear that some people have of flipping upside-down and getting trapped inside their boat. If for some reason you did capsize (which is surprisingly hard to do), you'd simply fall off the kayak.

Most contemporary SOTs are designed with a hatch for stowage in the bow. This gives you ample room to bring extra clothing, lunch, and spare rods and reels. Just aft of the cockpit, you might find tank wells for easy access storage of spare tackle, a cooler, or your catch. Sit-on-tops are also "self-bailing," meaning that water automatically drains out of the seat and off the deck through "scupper holes" that go right through the kayak. This means that unless your kayak suffers serious structural damage, you won't have to worry about swamping your boat.

There are a few downsides to SOTs that are worth considering. One is that they generally require more material than a SINK, so they tend to be a bit heavier. They are also usually wider than other kayaks, and although this makes them very stable, it also makes them less efficient to paddle. Another potential disadvantage is the fact that your lower body isn't protected, which means that you can expect your lower body to be wet when paddling an SOT, and exposed to the sun, wind and rain. This can be fine in warm environments, but if you're paddling in cold water, you'll need to wear clothing that will keep you warm even when it is wet.

One of the many benefits of a sit-on-top kayak is that you can sit and cast from a side-saddle position.

SIT-INSIDE KAYAKS (SINKS)

Sit-inside kayaks are more traditional and there are many to choose from. The best sit-inside kayaks for kayak fishing are found in the recreational category. Recreational sit-inside kayaks are recognizable by their big open cockpits, which makes them extremely safe and minimizes any fears that one might have of being trapped inside. In fact, the cockpits are so large that you will easily fall out if you capsize. Even the most experienced kayakers couldn't keep themselves inside to perform an Eskimo roll if they were to flip. Most SINKs also come with hatches in the bow and stern, which are semi-waterproof because of walls inside the kayak called bulkheads. These bulkheads divide the boat's interior into separate compartments, which not only helps keep a relatively dry spot for your gear, but provides flotation for your kayak in the event your cockpit is swamped.

The advantage of SINKs is that they allow you to stay far drier and protect your lower body from the sun and wind. You can even use a spray skirt to help keep water and sun off your legs.

The downsides of using sit-inside kayaks for fishing are that you don't have the same freedom to move around on your kayak that you do with a SOT, nor can you just hop in and out of them while on the water. Because sit-inside kayaks are not self-bailing, capsizing is also a much bigger issue because your boat will swamp.

The sit-inside kayak keeps you drier and protects your legs from sun and wind.

When deciding what type of kayak to buy, the most important question you need to answer is where you'll use it most of the time.

CHOOSING A KAYAK

When trying to decide what type of kayak will best suit your needs, the most important questions you can ask yourself are how and where you'll be using your kayak. For example, if you live in the south and want to go fishing on the shallow coastal flats where the water is warm and the weather warmer, or if you plan to fish anywhere that it's nice to have the option to quickly hop out of your kayak to wade fish, a sit-on-top will be the most practical choice. If you live in more northern or colder climates, or will be paddling in chillier water, a sit-inside might be the better boat for you.

Once you have decided on whether to go for a sit-on-top or sit-inside kayak, there are a few other issues to consider. As a general rule, the longer and narrower a boat is, the faster it will be. However, the wider a boat is, the more stable it will become, so narrower isn't necessarily better. Generally speaking, a short boat will be more maneuverable while a longer boat will track (go straight) more easily. Depending on where you'll spend

your time and what waters you want to fish, this could be a very important point to consider. For open water situations and paddling longer distances you might want to consider a longer kayak that is faster and tracks well. Should your fishing adventures take you to small creeks or rivers you would probably be better off with a shorter boat that will be easier to turn. Another factor to consider is that shorter boats are much easier to handle in transport and weigh considerably less than long ones. This can be an important consideration if you can foresee having to load your kayak by yourself.

What are Kayaks Made From?

The vast majority of kayaks used for kayak fishing have hard shells made from roto-molded polyethylene—more commonly known as "plastic". Plastic kayaks are very affordable, incredibly durable, and they require virtually no maintenance. The only downside to plastic kayaks is their weight. Thermoformed boats are relatively new to the market and are becoming somewhat more popular. The material used in the thermoforming process provides a great-looking kayak that is lighter, but it is not as resistant to impact as the roto-molded boats. Inflatable kayaks are made from coated fabrics and the best ones are more durable than most paddlers would imagine, but durability and puncturing are still a concern.

PADDLES

The paddle is one of the most important parts of the kayaking equation. It is the piece of equipment that translates your effort and energy into motion. Paddles come in a wide variety of shapes, sizes, and price ranges, so choosing one can be a daunting task for the beginner. If your kayak fishing excursions will keep you close to shore and close to where you started, almost any paddle will work. Just make sure that it is durable enough to stand up to the abuse that you will undoubtedly inflict upon it, and that it will effectively propel your kayak forward. However, if you will be traveling any real distance while kayak fishing, using a good quality paddle will make a big difference. The better paddles are lighter, stronger, and allow for more effective strokes, which will make your time on the water more comfortable and even more enjoyable. A lightweight, quality paddle also helps you avoid overuse injuries such as tendonitis in the wrist or elbow. As with most other sports these days, lighter equipment costs more money. Get the best paddle you can afford and you won't regret the extra dollars spent to shave those ounces.

Paddles have three main parts to them. They have a shaft, a power face and a back face. The majority of the shafts you will see are straight, but you will likely run across several models with shafts that are bent. Bent shafts are intended to be more ergonomically correct and provide the paddler with a more comfortable grip. Some models accomplish this goal better than others. The power face is the side of the paddle blade that catches water when you take a forward stroke. The back face is the side of the paddle that gets used for reverse strokes.

Kayak paddles are made from a variety of materials, although for casual paddling, plastic and fiberglass are by far the most common because they offer a great blend of performance, durability and affordability. The lowest priced paddles have an aluminum shaft and plastic blades. While these are adequate and will get the job done, they are often quite heavy and inefficient. The highest end paddles are made with carbon fiber and are very light, strong, and stiff. These qualities make them the most efficient and pleasant paddles to use.

In general, paddles are measured in centimeters and range between 210 cm and 250 cm (roughly 6½ ft to 8 ft). The proper length is chosen based on the paddlers height, arm length, and what feels most comfortable. Paddles between 220 cm and 235 cm are the most common and it's a fair bet that if you pick a paddle in this range you'll be happy with it. A paddle that is too short will not reach the water as well and your strokes will not get good purchase. A paddle that is too long will feel

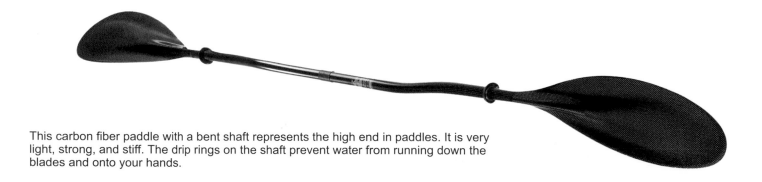

This carbon fiber paddle with a bent shaft represents the high end in paddles. It is very light, strong, and stiff. The drip rings on the shaft prevent water from running down the blades and onto your hands.

cumbersome and will tire you out more quickly.

One thing to consider is that a sit-on-top kayak is usually a bit wider than their sit-inside brethren. You also sit higher on them which means you have to reach a bit farther to the water. With this in mind you may want to err on the longer side if you're paddling a sit-on-top. We like to use 225 cm paddles when paddling sit-inside kayaks, and 235 cm paddles for our sit-on-tops.

Paddles also come with a variety of blade shapes and sizes. For kayak fishing, large blades are nice to have. The larger blades assist in the propulsion of the less efficient SOT kayaks and they help you turn your boat more quickly while maneuvering to fight a fish.

A final decision that you'll need to make has to do with the "feathering" of the paddle. A feathered paddle has blades that are offset from one another. This lets the upper blade slice through the air and wind more easily while taking a forward stroke. The downside is that it requires the paddler to twist the paddle while moving from one stroke to the next. Some people find that this causes fatigue or pain in their wrists. A paddle with no feather is much more intuitive to use and is a good choice for most kayak anglers. Most paddles come as two-piece designs that offer the option of being assembled with or without feathered blades. Something to note is that these two-piece adjustable paddles were designed to make paddles easier to transport, and to minimize the number of different paddles that stores needed to hold in inventory; not because you're supposed to adjust them all the time. Once you decide on, and become comfortable using a paddle with a certain degree of offset, we wouldn't recommend changing it around.

A paddle leash attaches your paddle to your boat so that you can't lose it while preoccupied, such as when you're fighting a fish.

TIP

If your kayak fishing ever takes you far from shore, into water that is subject to strong winds or current, or anywhere else where losing or breaking a paddle would mean you've got a serious problem, bring a spare paddle along. The spare can be easily and unobtrusively stowed under the elastic cord on the deck of your kayak or inside the kayak and out of the way.

PADDLE LEASHES

When you're fighting a fish in a kayak, it's easy to lose track of your gear and the paddle has an uncanny knack for taking advantage of the moment to make its getaway. Once the paddle is in the water, even though it's just a few yards away, you'd be surprised by how hard it can be to locate. Throw a little wind into the equation and that paddle can quickly disappear. To prevent this from happening, the paddle leash attaches your paddle to either you or your boat and is a good piece of security even if you're using a mounted paddle holder.

PFDS (PERSONAL FLOTATION DEVICES)

A PFD (lifejacket) is the single most important piece of equipment there is and should be worn whenever you're on the water. Of course, if it doesn't fit or isn't comfortable, then you probably won't wear it. On a similar note, if a PFD is worn improperly it can actually hinder your ability to swim rather than help. A good test for fit is to tighten the lifejacket as you would wear it, and then hook your thumbs under the shoulder straps and pull up. The jacket should stay in place on your torso and not lift in front of your face.

Any PFD that is Coast Guard Approved, fits well, and is comfortable enough so that you won't feel the need to remove it while on the water, is a perfectly adequate PFD. With that said, the best PFDs for kayak fishing are the ones that are designed specifically for the activity. There are now a number of kayak fishing PFDs to choose from. They all have a variety of pockets and keep the flotation away from the shoulders so they won't restrict your paddling or casting. Some have even removed the flotation from the lower back to accommodate the seats that many anglers use.

A kayak fishing specific PFD keeps the flotation away from the shoulders and chest so that you're not restricted when paddling or casting. It also has convenient pockets for gear.

SEATS

Sit-inside kayaks come with prefabricated seats that are installed and ready to use. A few models of sit-on-tops come equipped with a backrest, but most don't have anything more than the contoured seat pan. Although you can use these kayaks as they are, you can expect a mutiny from your butt and lower back within a short period of time. A simple back band that supports your lower back is an inexpensive and effective solution. However, the best seats will have foam for padding and high backrests that are fully adjustable and quite comfortable. Many of these types of seat will also have added features such as rod holders and detachable storage packs.

ROD HOLDERS

Although you have the option of simply stowing your rods inside your kayak, opening the hatch to access your rods while on the water can be somewhat difficult. For this reason, rod holders are one of the kayak angler's best friends. Not only do they let you paddle unencumbered and take quick action when you sight a fish, but they also offer you the opportunity to troll as you paddle along. Although some kayaks will come equipped with rod holders, there's a good chance that you'll need to install them. When doing so, you'll need to decide on the type of rod holder you'd like to use, where you'd like it positioned and how many you'll need. Obviously, how you'll be using your rod holder is what makes this decision. Does it need to place the rod at an angle suitable for trolling? Will you be setting out multiple baited rods? Or are you simply looking for a place to store your rod while you paddle?

Regarding the positioning of the rod holder, there is no "right" way, simply personal preference. With that said, in our opinion the rod holders are best installed behind your seat within easy reach. Having as little equipment as possible in the front of the kayak allows the most freedom while fishing. It's also nice to have the rods in the back and out of the way in case you fall out

The Surf to Summit kayak fishing seat is extremely comfortable, and has convenient rod holders and oversized pockets.

of your kayak and need to perform a deep water re-entry.

There are three common types of rod holders used by kayak anglers, all of which work well. Scotty makes an adjustable mounting style rod holder with a flush mount receiver that is simple, functional, and can be used for any of the purposes listed above. There are two styles of rod holder that both fit the same receiver. One is designed for fly or spinning gear while the other is designed with bait casters in mind. The bait caster version will also work for spinning reels, but it isn't ideal. One of the great features of these rod holders is that they can be removed from the kayak when not in use. As an added bonus, Scotty makes a 360 degree stern light that mounts into the same style receiver. Another surface mount style is made by Tite-lok. The rod holder will accept any style of rod and reel, and detaches for transport leaving only the flush-mounted base on the kayak.

The standard flush mount rod holder that is commonly seen in power boats also works very well. The hollow interior of kayaks makes mounting these holders quick and simple. The models intended for use in kayaks all come with the interior end capped and sealed, but there are some models intended for boats which are open on the end and that would allow any water splashing up onto the kayak to enter. Needless to say this is not ideal and you will want to cap it. The only downside to this type of rod holder is the fact that your reel is sitting on the deck of the kayak and is much closer to the water. This isn't a huge deal in freshwater, but it will take its toll on your equipment if you're fishing in saltwater. Some kayak anglers have used their creativity to get around this problem by fashioning extenders out of PVC pipe that raise the reel higher off the water. As a side note, this style of rod holder also offers a great place to stow an anchor for quick deployment.

A final popular method for storing extra rods is to mount PVC pipe into a milk crate or a small ice chest, which can then be stored in the rear tankwell of a sit-on-top kayak. Using this technique, you can carry a variety of rods rigged and ready to go, so you can deal with almost any opportunity that pops up. The disadvantage to this style of rod holder is that your rods are stored further back in the tankwell and you'll likely need to

If you plan on trolling, you'll want a rod holder mounted securely in front of you.

Some kayak anglers use PVC piping and a milk crate secured in the tank well of the kayak to act as rod holders and storage.

either sit side-saddle or get out of your kayak to access the rods. This isn't a big deal in shallow water situations, but in rough or deep water it will be more difficult.

PADDLE HOLDERS

Most of the popular sit-on-top fishing kayaks come equipped with some type of built-in paddle holder, which lets you quickly stow your paddle along the side of your kayak and out of the way so that you can cast or fight a fish unimpeded. Some paddle holders use a small piece of bungee cord that loops over the paddle shaft to hold the paddle in place, while paddle clips allow you to simply snap your paddle in and out. Although both styles work well, and we find they come in handy at times, we'll usually just slide our paddle under the cargo bungee cords at the bow of our kayak. This is a quick and easy way to store your paddle and with practice it can be done quietly.

If your kayak doesn't have a paddle holder or cargo bungee cords at the bow, both are things that you can install. Something to keep in mind is that if you plan to sit and cast from a side-saddle position in a sit-on-top, then you'll want to set this up on your off-side so that it is usually out of your way. (For more information about this, see the section on "Side-Saddle Fishing" in Chapter 4.)

ANCHORS

Anchors for kayak fishing are used in the same way that they are when fishing from a power boat. You'll either set an anchor to hold yourself in place, or use an anchor to slow the speed at which wind pushes you across the water. There are a couple of different styles of anchors that are common and effective for kayak fishing, depending on their desired purpose and the type of bottom you'll be fishing over.

Probably the most common type of anchor used for kayak fishing is the folding anchor. These grapple-hook style anchors have three or four points that fold out when in use and that can be folded up and secured while stowed. These anchors seem to work best on soft bottoms or in heavy vegetation, but

Paddle clips allow the paddle to be stored comfortably and easily along the side of the kayak.

The folding anchor is popular with kayak anglers, and works really well on soft bottoms or in heavy vegetation.

they don't work as well on hard or sandy bottoms. As a bonus, the folding anchor can be used in its stored position to simply create drag for a more controlled drift.

A lesser-known type of anchor that works great for kayaks is the Bruce anchor, which resembles a plow and works in much the same way. A 2.2 pound Bruce anchor will securely hold a kayak in almost any condition and with any type of bottom, short of solid rock.

For drift fishing (see Chapter 4), there are a number of anchors that one can use. The most common techniques involve dragging some type of weight that won't snag along the bottom, or else using a parachute style anchor that slows you down by catching water. An 18 – 24" diameter parachute will be enough to slow you down in any wind that's safe to fish and paddle, and you can find them in marine supply and tackle stores. It's a good idea to get a parachute made from a brightly colored material so that you can easily locate it. This will come in handy when you're battling a fish, many of which seem to have an uncanny ability to wrap a fishing line around the trailing drift anchor or its rope.

Whichever type of anchor you use, an important part of the anchoring system is the rope itself. A kayak doesn't require the same size of rope that a power boat anchor uses. A 1/4" to 3/8" braided nylon rope will work just fine and if it's a soft, braided nylon, it will be easier on your wet hands. Of course, you'll want to occasionally examine the condition of the rope and its knots because anchor failure can get you in real trouble if it happens at the wrong time. It's also highly recommended that you have a knife handy that is capable of easily cutting through your anchor rope, should the need arise.

There are a few other accessories that can come in handy. A small brass clip on the end of the anchor rope works well for securing it to various points on the kayak. It's also a good idea to attach a large, brightly colored float to the rope near the clip so that if you need to release the anchor while fighting a fish, you can relocate it afterwards. For a parachute anchor, this float will also keep the chute near the surface and away from bottom snags. In deeper water or in rough conditions, it may also become necessary to attach a short length of chain

to the anchor to help it find purchase on the bottom.

Once you've decided on a type of anchor, your next decision has to do with how you'll attach the anchor rope to your kayak. There are numerous ways to do so, which range from simply clipping the anchor line to a secure point on your boat, to some fairly complicated trolley systems that allow the user to anchor from any point along the kayak between the bow and stern. The most common type of trolley consists of a pulley at either end of the kayak with a loop of rope running through them and alongside the kayak. A ring for attaching the anchor line is built into the loop of rope. The kayak can then be positioned by moving the location of the connection ring between the pulleys and then securing the rope in place. The advantage of this trolley system is that in current and wind you can control the position of your boat while it's anchored. The disadvantage of the trolley system is that ropes running down the sides clutter up the kayak and create an opportunity for you or your gear to get entangled. Since we prefer to have as little gear around or in front of us as possible, we like to clip our anchor line to a pad eye located on the side of the kayak, just behind the seat, but again, this is a matter of personal preference.

The storage of your anchor is an important consideration. It needs to be located somewhere that is easy to access and yet out of the way. The anchor line also needs to be clear of obstructions that will hinder the deployment of the anchor. With a sit-on-top, this can be accomplished by placing the anchor and extra rope towards the front of the rear tankwell or in a milk crate.

STOWAGE

Most kayaks have some sort of built-in storage. For a sit-on-top, it's the entire interior of the kayak; for a sit-inside it's a compartmentalized area in the front and/or rear portions of the kayak. Although these compartments are supposed to be waterproof, there has yet to be designed a kayak storage compartment that doesn't experience some leakage. The most common causes of water penetration are waves splashing

The tank well of a sit-on-top kayak offers lots of "wet" storage space. Anything that needs to stay dry should be in proper dry bags with a waterproof seal.

over the hatches, or the kayak momentarily submerging while traversing large waves. Keep anything that needs to stay dry in waterproof containers in the storage compartments. Dry bags work really well, as do hard-shell dry cases such as Pelican boxes. We often see new kayakers using common sandwich type or zip-lock baggies to store their cell phones or cameras and it has cost them on more than one occasion. Go ahead and splurge on the real deal. Get yourself a quality dry bag or box.

FISH FINDERS AND DEPTH SOUNDERS

Although far from being an essential piece of equipment for kayak fishing, more and more fish finders and depth sounders are finding their way onto kayaks. If you're interested in rigging your kayak with either, you'll want to find the smallest units possible to get the job done. The transducers can be mounted inside the hull using an epoxy or heavy-duty silicon sealant/adhesive. The process can be tricky and getting good accurate readings from your unit depends on your attention to detail. Small rechargeable gel-cell batteries are the most common source of power, and a small fish finder can be run all day on a full charge.

THIGH STRAPS

Thigh straps are an extra that provide added control for sit-on-top kayaks and only need to be considered for paddling in more challenging conditions, such as when paddling out through surf. For this reason, the vast majority of kayak anglers will never need thigh straps.

SPRAY SKIRT

The spray skirt, or spray deck, covers the cockpit of a sit-inside kayak. For traditional kayaking, the skirt is designed to keep all water out of your boat, but for recreational kayaks (like kayak fishing boats), the skirt is usually made of a lighter material, and can be used to help keep water from splashing into your kayak and/or to help keep the sun off your legs. Skirts are definitely not

an essential piece of gear for kayak fishing in sit-inside kayaks, but they can be helpful at times. You can even get a mini spray skirt, which only covers the cockpit in front of your body. This makes them a much cooler option and offers the angler a nice platform for either stripping fly line or having lunch.

RUDDERS

Although this may come as a surprise, kayak rudders were not designed to make the boat turn. They're designed to help your kayak "track"—which means travel in a straight line.

Most of the fishing kayaks over 12 feet now come with a molded-in rudder mount in the stern, although there may not actually be a rudder. If the boat does have a rudder mount but no rudder, you can have one installed if you decide that you need one.

Rudders flip down from their stored position on deck by means of haul lines found along the side of the kayak. Unlike skegs, rudders swivel side to side and are controlled by foot pedals. The downside of rudders is that you can expect them to add $150 - $200 to the cost of your kayak, and they are subject to more damage than any other part of your boat.

INSTALLING ACCESSORIES

One of the cool things about getting into kayak fishing is rigging your boat. Nothing helps beat the winter blues better than tinkering with your kayak and dreaming of the coming spring. Polyethylene kayaks are easy to work on with basic tools. The only tools you'll need that may not be found in your typical garage are a variable-sized hole saw and a pop rivet tool. These are easy to find and fairly inexpensive to acquire.

In general, we try to avoid using rivets because it's hard to trust them to bear any type of load, and of course having a rivet pull out of your kayak while on the water is a headache that no one wants to deal with. Locking nuts, washers, and bolts are the best for attaching anything that will have to take a load, but these will be difficult to use if your kayak doesn't

Every angler has their own tricks. Brendan uses his mounted fillet board.

allow access to its interior. If this is your situation, rivets or well nuts are your only choices, but we wouldn't recommend using well nuts on anything that will have even minimal stress placed upon it. If a well nut pulls out you'll have a half-inch hole to deal with, which is far from ideal if you're on the water. When using rivets, be sure to get the type that flare out equally all the way around to more evenly disperse the load. They aren't easy to find, but they are worth the effort because they do a much better job than standard rivets.

On a final note, everything that gets mounted to your kayak should get a liberal application of silicone sealant. The excess silicone can be removed with WD-40 and a rag.

CLOTHING

DRESSING FOR WARM WATER CONDITIONS

When the water is warm and the air temperature is even warmer, dressing properly for a day out on the water is easy. Your biggest concerns are staying protected from the sun's harmful rays and keeping hydrated. Of course, the best solution is to cover up and use sunscreen on any exposed skin. Even on the hottest day, a lightweight long sleeve shirt and long pants such as those made by Ex-Officio are a good idea because they keep the sun off the arms and body. There are some great quick-drying, ultra-light materials on the market that provide a good balance of sun protection and coolness. For those using a sit-inside kayak, a mini spray skirt is a good option. Because the mini-skirt only covers the front part of the cockpit, it keeps the sun off your lower extremities without turning your kayak into a sweat box. On the feet, a good pair of water shoes or sandals like Tevas will always come in handy, although some areas warrant additional foot protection, especially if you plan to step off your kayak and wade fish.

Quality sunglasses are another important means of protecting yourself from the sun, particularly early or late in the day when the sun's glare off the water can be blinding. Get sunglasses that are polarized and provide good UV protection. The UV light rays are very harmful to your eyes. Of course, you'll want to have some type of retainer strap so that they can't fall into the water.

DRESSING FOR COLD WATER CONDITIONS

When the air is warm and the water is cold, dressing appropriately can be a real challenge. No matter how warm the air is, swimming in cold water can drop your core body temperature to hypothermic levels at an alarming rate. On the flip side, being over dressed in hot weather can result in heat stroke. The key is dressing in a way that keeps you

In warm climates, sun protection will be your main concern when deciding what to wear.

A farmer john wetsuit is good and affordable protection from cold water.

A waterproof and windproof jacket is important for staying dry and warm.

cool enough when things are going well, yet warm enough in the event of a capsize. A neoprene wetsuit is one of the best options for these conditions. A neoprene farmer john provides good insulation for a modest price and the cut of the garment allows a full range of movement in the shoulder without chafing. A wetsuit is a great foundation piece for your paddling wardrobe because as temperatures drop, you can add more clothing for more warmth.

When both the water and the air temperature are cold, hypothermia becomes a serious hazard. You need to wear clothing that insulates well, both when dry and wet. This is where materials like fleece, polypropylene and neoprene excel. Cotton is the worst option. Cotton dries very slowly and rather than insulate, it actually pulls heat away from your body. Wool is another good option, although it gets really heavy when it's wet and takes forever to dry.

Over your insulating layers, you'll likely want to have an outer layer that keeps the wind off your body. Waterproof nylon jacket and pants work well. For your feet, try neoprene booties and a pair of wool socks. The ultimate outer-layer protection against the cold is a dry suit. A dry suit uses latex gaskets at the ankles, wrists and neck to keep all water out, even when you're completely immersed. Dry suits are expensive, but if you spend a lot of time paddling in cold conditions it will be a great investment in terms of both comfort and safety.

Of course, the best strategy of all is to avoid capsizing altogether. By paddling in protected areas and fishing conservatively, capsizing is highly unlikely. Fishing kayaks are so stable that as long as you're paddling in a sheltered area that

isn't subject to strong wind or waves, there's no reason to flip. As an added precaution, it's also important that you stay close to shore, so that in the unlikely event that you capsize, you can quickly swim to safety while your fishing buddies gather your equipment—when they're done laughing. The type of boat that you're paddling will also dictate how you'll need to dress in cold water. If you're paddling a sit-on-top kayak, you should prepare for your lower body to get wet, whereas a sit-inside will provide far more protection from the elements.

There are a number of other pieces of clothing that come in handy, and most kayaks have plenty of room to bring extra gear along. A wooly hat is a great addition on a chilly day, as are neoprene gloves, both of which will keep insulating if they get damp or wet. If you're using a sit-inside kayak, you can also wear a spray skirt to keep cold water out of your boat and allow your body heat to warm up the interior of the cockpit. Do yourself a favor and bring along a change of clothes stored in a dry bag. Should you unexpectedly become soaked on a cold day, you'll really appreciate this little nugget of advice.

Many people chose to wear waders to stay completely dry while kayaking. This is not a bad option, but it does require some fore-thought from a safety aspect. Waders full of water are very difficult to move around in and capsizing in deep water then becomes potentially deadly. To combat large amounts of water getting inside your waders you can wear a snug fitting wading belt around the upper portion of the waders. This generally won't stop all of the water from entering, but it will slow the process down quite a bit giving you more time to react and get yourself out of the bad situation.

SAFETY GEAR

Although kayak fishing is generally a very safe activity, as with anything, there is always the potential for things to go wrong. If things do go awry, having the equipment on hand to quickly and efficiently deal with the situation can make a huge difference. As a general rule, if there's even a chance that you could use something, then bring it along. Fishing kayaks have a lot of cargo space and so there's no reason not to, and as Murphy's Law states: if you don't bring it, you're going to need it.

The following is a list of basic safety equipment. Of course, every situation is different and so before every trip you'll need to decide on what combination of safety gear makes the most sense. If you're just heading out on a small protected lake for a quick after-work outing, you won't need much in the way of safety gear. Your best piece of safety equipment is your PFD, so make sure you're wearing it at all times. It's also a good idea to always bring a whistle.

On the other hand, if you plan on making a more adventuresome trip you might want to consider bringing a full complement of safety gear. These situations may include trips where you'll be paddling farther from shore than you can comfortably swim, venturing along rugged shorelines that don't provide easy escape from the water, or if the possibility exists that you will have to deal with waves, wind or current. Remember too that safety equipment doesn't do any good if you don't know how to use it. So, if you want to fish in unsheltered, open water, especially with a sit-inside kayak (since you can't just hop back into it if you flip), you should consider getting professional instruction on kayak safety and rescue.

WATER AND ENERGY BARS

It might not be something that you would consider as safety gear, but since your body is the engine that drives your kayak forward, it's essential that it get enough fuel to do the job. Arguably more important than food is water. Staying hydrated will keep you warm and happily fishing all day long.

FIRST AID KIT

For obvious reasons, a first aid kit is always a good idea to bring along and there are some great ready-to-go kits available. Beyond the basic bandages and wound cleansers, make sure the kit includes elastic wraps, plenty of heavy gauze pads and a good waterproof tape. Be sure to throw your first aid kit into a dry bag before tossing it into your boat.

EMERGENCY BAG

Most of us never think we are going to get stranded out for the night, and though rare, it happens. If you are going to be fishing in a remote area from which you can't easily walk out, an emergency bag is a good piece of insurance to bring along. Some food, a headlamp and some extra clothing can make what would otherwise be a miserable experience into a tolerable adventure. In cold weather you may want to consider placing something in your pack to assist you in starting a fire.

SPARE PADDLE

No matter how well-built your paddle is, there is always a chance it could break or get lost. A spare paddle is simply a must if you are fishing in areas that don't leave you with any options other than paddling home. In a group setting, not every angler needs to have a spare paddle, but there should be at least one spare per group.

PADDLE FLOATS

Paddle floats provide the opportunity to re-enter a capsized sit-inside kayak without anyone's help. The paddle float attaches to your paddle blade and allows the paddle to be used as an outrigger to stabilize the boat as you get back in. Although they have the potential of being useful, they require training and practice to use. The better option is to avoid paddling alone so that you always have a buddy who can support your kayak while you re-enter.

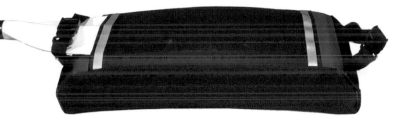

BILGE PUMPS

Kayak bilge pumps are mostly manual hand-held models. They are only necessary for sit-inside kayaks, which will swamp if they capsize. If you paddle a sit-inside and venture into waters too deep to wade to safety, then you should carry a pump.

COMMUNICATION DEVICES

Communication devices are tools that can help you stay in contact or help manage difficult situations. Of course, they're also great for calling others in your party to see if they're having any luck where they are, or to brag about the fish that you just landed. There are several communication devices available to the kayak angler.

Cell Phones

Cell phones are a great item to have along. Make sure the batteries are charged and you have adequate cell coverage everywhere you'll be going. Keeping a cell phone dry is a challenge, so you'll want to carry them in a quality dry

If you're going to rely on a cell phone for communication, make sure the batteries are charged and that you have service in the area.

storage of some sort. There are even small dry bags designed specifically for cell phones that let you use them while they stay protected inside. Keep in mind that even the slightest amount of moisture can wreck a phone.

VHF Radios

An important piece of safety equipment when traveling any distance on the ocean or on very large lakes is a handheld VHF radio, because they can reach other boats in the area as well as the Coast Guard. You can also listen to an up-to-date weather report. Something to note about VHF radios is that there is a strict and established protocol for their use, which is designed to reduce channel overcrowding and to keep specific channels open to distress calls, so if you want to use one, be sure you know the rules.

SIGNALING DEVICES

Signaling devices are used to get attention and are usually reserved for emergencies.

Whistles

A whistle can be heard much more easily and over a greater distance than simply yelling. A small hand-held air horn is even louder. Because they are so small, versatile and effective, we recommend that you bring a whistle every time you go out in your boat. An easy way to carry it is to attach it to your PFD or stick it in a PFD pocket.

Strobes

A strobe is a very bright flashing light. Strobes can be attached to the shoulder of your PFD to attract attention at night or in low light, but they should only be activated in an emergency, because on the water a flashing strobe represents a mayday signal.

Flares and Smoke

Flares at night and smoke during the day can mean the difference between being found or remaining lost. Both are readily available at any marine supply store. There are also dye packs that can be deployed. These dye packs create a huge brightly colored cloud on the water's surface to attract the attention of rescue aircraft.

Reflectors

You should always carry some sort of reflector along for signaling. A small mirror or a CD will do the job.

NAVIGATION TOOLS

Navigation tools are pieces of equipment that help you establish where you are on the water and how to get to where you want to be. Basic navigation is something that we all do instinctively (some better than others), and in many cases you won't need any real tools. For example, if you're lost on a lake you'll know that by following the shoreline one way or another, eventually you'll get back to where you started. Similarly, it is pretty straight forward when fishing on a river. You'll know that if you paddled upstream to begin with, heading downstream on that same side of the river will get you back home. On the ocean or other large bodies of water, if you stick to one shoreline you can just turn around and head back home at any point. Although navigation tools aren't necessary in these cases, when you start dealing with more complicated marine geography they quickly become essential. Just buying the equipment isn't enough. Spend some time learning the skills to use these tools and you'll be much more confident when you set out. If you want to fish in more remote areas, you'll want to take a course in navigation. Here is a quick overview of some of the more important navigation tools that you can learn to use.

Charts

Nautical charts are basically maps that focus on the marine environment. When buying charts for an area, you'll have to consider what scale is most useful to you. If you intend to get any fishing done, then you probably won't be covering a huge amount of ground and so small-scale charts will be your best option. To carry the charts, you'll need a waterproof chart case.

In areas prone to getting fog, a chart and compass can be your best friends.

GPS units

Handheld global positioning system (GPS) units are incredible pieces of technology that can tell you where you are to within a few feet. Data from satellites is used to triangulate your location. Some even have charts built into the unit that will show you exactly where you are on the map. GPS units are very handy for locating specific fishing locations and mapping out routes to those special places. They're also pretty nice to have when the bite is on and darkness sneaks up on you. When you're focused on the fish, it's easy to get disoriented and a GPS will help you get back to your vehicle. Basic units are relatively inexpensive and very compact. The only problem with GPS units is that they rely entirely on batteries. Like any other piece of electronic equipment, they are subject to failure in the field. For this reason, you don't want to ever be solely reliant on them. If navigation tools may come in handy, bring a reliable backup like a compass and chart.

Compasses

The magnetic compass is another key navigation tool, but of course, they're only useful if you know how to use them. The best compasses for kayak fishing are hand-held and waterproof. There are also deck mounted models available, but they tend to get in the way when mounted on the forward deck.

Tide and Current Tables

Tides and currents can both have profound effects on sea conditions. Happily, both tides and tidal currents can be predicted with reasonable accuracy using tide and current tables, along with the appropriate marine charts.

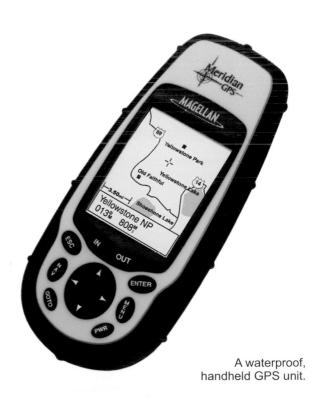

A waterproof, handheld GPS unit.

Care and Maintenance for
Your Kayak and Gear

Transporting Your Kayak

Carrying Your Kayak

Packing Your Kayak

Getting In and Out of
Your Kayak

Sitting In a Kayak

Using Your Paddle

Using Rudders or Skegs

Choosing a Kayak Fishing

Location

BEFORE HITTING THE WATER

THE WATER

chapter two

2

CARE AND MAINTENANCE FOR YOUR KAYAK AND GEAR

Kayaks are extremely simple and low maintenance watercraft, especially when compared to powerboats. However, there are a few ways that you can prolong the life of your kayak and maintain its overall appearance and performance.

One of the most common ways to damage a kayak is to store it improperly. There are a few good ways to store a kayak. You can lean it up on its side, cradle it with hanging straps, or you can sit it on a padded rack that supports the bow and stern. Regardless of how you store it, make sure that you remove any water or extra gear from inside as the additional weight can cause the hull of the kayak to deform. It's also important that you keep your kayak out of the sun as much as possible. The sun's powerful UV rays will dull its color and make the material more brittle and subject to cracking.

Saltwater can also takes its toll on a kayak and your gear over time, but a simple freshwater rinse will take care of that. Pay particular attention to any metal parts such as rudders and their cables, deck cleats and any other moving parts such as foot pegs.

Something to note is that it is normal for the hull of plastic kayaks to deform a bit over time, but unless the deformity is major it should have virtually no impact on your kayak's performance. If the boat is showing serious warping or dents, a little heat will often be enough to return the kayak to its original shape. On a hot day, leaving your kayak in the sun for a little while will often be enough to pop out the dents. If that doesn't work, you can dump some hot water into the kayak and use your hands (don't burn yourself!) to encourage some of the dents to pop out.

With enough force (and it takes a lot), it's possible to crack or puncture a kayak, which is obviously a serious problem. Composite boats with this kind of damage can be repaired quite easily by someone who is experienced in fiberglass work. Plastic boats can be repaired through careful use of a heating source and some spare plastic. It is a good idea to keep any cut-outs or drill bit shavings for future use in any patching jobs that may arise.

The ideal roof racks for transporting kayaks are specifically designed for the purpose. Factory-installed roof racks aren't usually reliable or strong enough.

TRANSPORTING YOUR KAYAK

Not surprisingly, one of the most common questions we field at boat shows, demo days, and kayak symposiums has to do with transporting kayaks. It's a valid concern, because transporting a 10 to 16-foot boat does take a game plan and it's not something that you want to mess up. Losing a kayak on the freeway is as dangerous as it gets; maybe not for you, but for the other drivers on the road.

There are basically three options for transporting fishing kayaks. You can tie your boat onto a roof rack, tow the kayak on a trailer, or if you have a pick-up, you can simply tie the kayak into the bed of the truck. If you're going to tie the kayak into the bed of your truck, don't forget that in most areas you are required to put a red flag on anything that extends more than four feet beyond the rear of the vehicle. This requirement may vary so check your state and local regulations to be sure.

The nice thing about trailers is that loading them is generally very easy and you'll usually be able to carry several kayaks at the same time. With some creativity, you can take a trailer designed for a powerboat and make a few small modifications that will allow it to carry kayaks. The downside is trailer storage, registration fees, and maintenance will be required.

Roof racks are by far the most popular method of transporting kayaks and there are models available to accommodate almost any vehicle. Unfortunately, factory-installed racks are seldom strong enough to transport kayaks, so you'll need to consider an alternative. The cheapest option is to use simple foam blocks that sit on the roof of your vehicle. You'll then strap the kayak down to your car using cam straps threaded through your vehicle. Although this can do the trick for short trips, the ideal roof racks are those like the ones that Thule (www.thule.com) offers. Thule has rack systems for every type of vehicle as well as ones that are specifically designed for carrying kayaks. They are all designed to be mounted on your vehicle and can be purchased with a mechanism that locks the racks to your vehicle. Another great option for kayak anglers are boat cradles and kayak rollers. Boat cradles mount onto the racks and cup your boat. This holds them in place and spreads the load when you tie the kayak down, which helps prevent deformation of the hull. Kayak rollers have wheels that help you slide the boat onto your vehicle from behind, making

loading and unloading easier. Whatever type of roof rack that you use, it's always a good idea to tie bow and stern lines to the front and back of your vehicle to help stabilize the kayak and prevent it from shooting off like a torpedo if you need to brake quickly.

CARRYING YOUR KAYAK

Although there are a lot of benefits to using a plastic kayak, weight isn't one of them. Plastic kayaks tend to be somewhat heavy, which can make carrying them a bit of a pain. The best way to carry a boat from your vehicle to shore is the buddy system, with one person holding the grab loop at each end. Many fishing kayaks come with a grab handle along the side of the boat for carrying it suitcase style. While this works, you probably won't want to carry your kayak for long distances using this method. If you're alone,

Lift the kayak onto your thighs with the cockpit out.

Grab the far edge, thumb out, with the hand that is on the same side as the shoulder that the boat will sit on.

it might be best to drag the kayak to the shoreline, but be careful of the type of surface you'll be traversing. Concrete, asphalt and rocky shorelines are going to take a toll on your boat.

Sit-inside kayaks also offer the opportunity to shoulder-carry the kayak, although getting it onto your shoulder can be a challenge on its own. When doing so, make sure you bend your legs and keep your back as straight as possible. Start by grabbing the close side of the cockpit coaming and then lifting the boat onto your thighs so that the cockpit is facing outwards. You'll then grab the far edge of the coaming, and roll the boat up and onto your shoulder. To put the kayak back down, reverse these steps.

Another great option if you need to carry your kayak any distance is a kayak cart. Kayak carts have two wheels and support the kayak at either the end or in the middle. Most carts pack down on the top deck of a kayak or inside the hull.

Only experience will teach you the best way to pack your kayak for the greatest efficiency for your style of fishing. When starting out, just remember to keep close at hand the things that you're going to want quick access to. You don't want to have to search for things like flies and lures, water bottles, or your net. Also keep in mind that certain areas will be inaccessible when you're on the water and will require that you land and get out of your kayak to gain access. These less accessible spots are great places for things like foul weather gear, a first aid kit, or an emergency kit.

One fairly popular piece of equipment for packing a sit-on-top kayak is the milk crate. A milk crate fits in the rear tankwell of most common fishing style sit-on-top kayaks. They can be

Use your knee
to kick the boat up and roll it up onto your shoulder.

To recover your paddle you can use
your foot or squat, keeping your back straight.

Most sit-on-top kayaks have tank wells in the back that can carry a lot of gear, although anything that can't get wet will need to be put in proper dry bags.

strapped down very easily and provide quick access to a lot of different gear.

Anything that can't get wet will need to be stored in a dry bag, and any loose gear that can sink should be tied to the kayak.

A few times out on the water and you'll quickly learn the art of packing your boat. As you gain more experience, you will undoubtedly find yourself shifting the gear around to suit your style. And just when you think you've discovered the best system, you'll run into someone who has an even better idea. This is one of the great things about kayak fishing tournaments. They provide you with the opportunity to see what other people are doing and get ideas that will help you make the most of your time on the water. The most important thing to remember is to try to distribute your gear evenly around the boat. An even weight distribution will help you get the best performance from your kayak.

GETTING IN AND OUT OF YOUR KAYAK

The easiest spots to get into and out of your kayak are beaches or flat areas where you can walk your kayak into the water, straddle it and then sit down. When doing this, one end of your boat will often remain on land and so you may need to

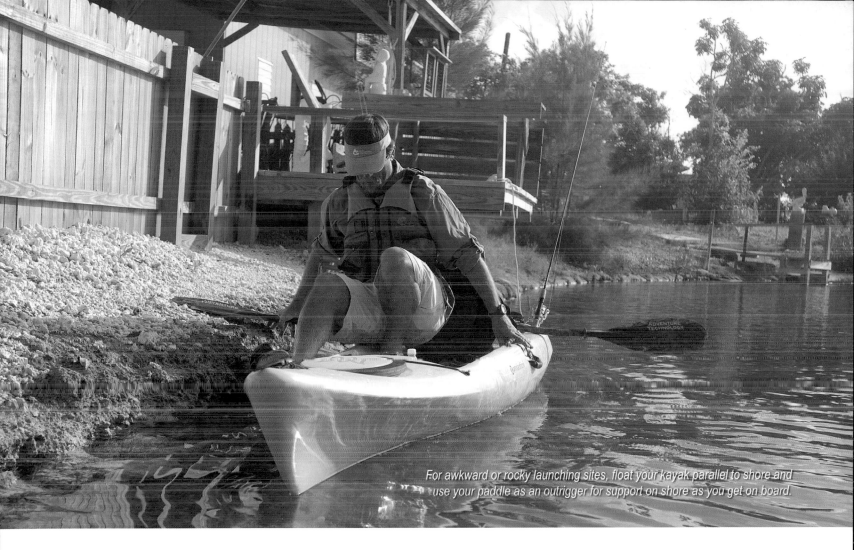

For awkward or rocky launching sites, float your kayak parallel to shore and use your paddle as an outrigger for support on shore as you get on board.

push off with your hands. If you push off with your paddle, push directly down the length of the shaft to avoid breaking a paddle blade.

Unfortunately, launch sites aren't always so convenient. In particular, docks and rocky shorelines can be tricky. With a little technique and practice, you'll be able to launch from all sorts of different places. The freedom to launch virtually anywhere is one of the huge advantages of kayak fishing.

If you find yourself needing to launch from a dock, choose the dock's lowest point. The higher the dock, the more chance you have to find yourself swimming. Start by positioning your kayak parallel to the dock and then sit down on the dock beside the kayak seat. Place your paddle close by

so that it will be within easy reach once you are in your boat. Next, put your feet in the kayak close to the centerline of the boat for maximum stability. Now turn your body towards the bow of the kayak, securing a good grip with both hands on the dock, and then lower yourself decisively into the seat. It's this awkward transition from sitting on the dock to sitting in the kayak where most of the carnage takes place, so be quick about getting your butt into the seat. To get out, you can simply reverse these steps.

For awkward or rocky launch sites, the best way to get into your boat is to float your kayak in the water, and then use your paddle as an outrigger for support. Place your paddle at 90 degrees to the kayak with the shaft resting on the boat just behind the cockpit and the far blade supported on the shore. Grasp the paddle shaft behind your back and squat down beside the kayak. While cheating your weight onto the outrigger, slip your legs into the boat and drop your butt into the seat. You can get out of your kayak on uneven or rocky shorelines using this same technique in reverse, although it will be difficult if you have any waves to contend with.

Something to consider after a long day on the water, particularly if you haven't stood up in awhile, is that your legs may not do everything that you want them to. An all too familiar and funny scene involves an angler stepping out of their kayak and then falling straight back into the water because their legs simply won't respond. Save yourself the embarrassment—take a moment to plan your exit and give your legs a good shake before you hop out.

SITTING IN A KAYAK

The seats designed for fishing kayaks are largely designed to make sitting comfortable and are not necessarily designed to hold your body in a good paddling position. Since you'll be spending a large part of your time sitting and casting, this certainly isn't a bad thing, but you should be aware of how you need to be sitting in a kayak when you're paddling. Good posture in a boat will allow you to paddle more comfortably, promote more efficient strokes and help you avoid back pain.

The ideal position for paddling a kayak is to sit up straight with your feet resting against the foot pedals or in the foot wells so that your knees are bent and somewhat splayed out. Look at it this way. Try sitting on your living room floor to watch your favorite half hour sitcom with your legs straight out in front

Although there's nothing wrong with kicking back and lounging in a kayak, to avoid back pain it's important to sit upright while actively paddling.

As a right-handed paddler, Joel's right hand has a firm grip on the paddle as he takes a stroke on the right, while his left hand stays loose.

of you with knees touching. You won't make it. You'll naturally lift your knees, splay your legs and draw your feet towards you for relief. It shouldn't be surprising that this is the proper paddling position. If you have trouble sitting like this on the floor or in your boat, it's probably because your hamstrings are too tight. Now, most anglers we know probably wouldn't adhere to a specific stretching routine, nor do they show much interest in yoga. However, it is important to note that improving your flexibility will make sitting in a kayak a lot more comfortable. So it is worth at least taking a minute or two to do some toe touching (or as close as you can get!) at the put in.

Now there's more to sitting in the kayak than the proper paddling position. Particularly when kayak fishing, you spend more time moving around the boat getting a piece of gear or tying on a new lure over the course of a day than you do paddling. There's really no right or wrong way to do this. Just proceed with caution and move slowly until you get the hang of it. With experience, your balance and confidence will increase to the point that you will be able to move about quite freely.

USING YOUR PADDLE

In the next chapter we'll be taking an in-depth look at the various strokes and paddling techniques, but for now we're going to look at the basics of using a paddle. Not only will this let you make the most of your strokes, but it will help you avoid overuse injuries such as tendonitis in the wrist or elbow.

A kayak paddle should be held with your hands an equal distance from the blades and slightly more than shoulder width apart. A great way to establish the correct hand placement is to position the center of the paddle on top of your head and then grip the paddle so that your elbows are bent at approximately 90 degrees.

Knowing roughly where your hands should be, the next thing to look at is whether or not your paddle has any feather to contend with. Feathered paddles have blades offset at different angles. As one blade pulls through the water, the angle of the other blade allows it to slice through any wind. Feathered paddles

If the right hand is the control hand, it should retain a firm grip with the big knuckles aligned with the top edge of the paddle blade.

The left hand stays loose so that after a stroke on the right is taken, the shaft can rotate in the left hand so the left blade can be planted squarely in the water.

are traditional and can make a small difference if you're paddling in an area with high winds, but they are less intuitive to use and by no means essential. You may want to try both feathered and unfeathered paddles and decide on which you prefer. Let's start by taking a look at how to use a feathered paddle, since it is a useful concept to understand whether your paddle is feathered or not.

First off, you need to decide which hand will be your "control" hand. In general, if you are right-handed, your right hand will be your control hand. Likewise the left hand will be the control hand for left-handed paddlers. Your control hand keeps a firm grip on the shaft at all times which is why it is also referred to as the "glue" hand. The opposite hand, in contrast, is often referred to as the "grease" hand. The control hand's grip should never change whether you're forward paddling, back paddling, or performing any other stroke. The big knuckles of your control hand should be aligned with the top edge of your paddle blade. After taking a stroke with your

control hand side, you'll loosen your grip with your grease hand so that you can rotate the shaft within it. This rotation is necessary to accommodate the feather of your paddle and lets you place the next blade in the water squarely. This loosening of the grease hand and the rotation of the shaft within it takes place between each stroke.

If you're using a paddle with no feather you can get away with not rotating the paddle between each stroke. However it is ideal to use this same technique in a scaled-back way because there is naturally a small amount of rotation associated with paddling. If you don't let the paddle shaft rotate a little in your grease hand, you'll find that wrist doing small curls while you paddle, which can gradually result in an injury or strain.

On a final note, it's important that you keep your control hand grip on the paddle secure, but as light as possible. Certainly don't white-knuckle it. A light grip will let you paddle more comfortably for longer and is instrumental for avoiding overuse injuries such as tendonitis in the wrist and elbow.

Rudders are really convenient for kayak fishing because they let you steer the boat with your feet, leaving your hands free to catch fish.

USING RUDDERS OR SKEGS

The main purpose of rudders and skegs is to keep a kayak going straight when paddling in wind. When moving forward, a kayak will naturally turn into the wind, or "weather-cock". By using a rudder or skeg you can counteract this. Without a rudder or skeg, you might find yourself needing more powerful strokes on the windward side and virtually no strokes on the leeward side of your kayak. Over a long distance this can make travel exhausting, not to mention very inefficient.

Because rudders swivel side-to-side (unlike skegs), they are much more powerful for controlling a kayak and also much more popular than skegs for kayak fishing. Rudders flip down from

their stored position on top of the deck using haul lines that are found alongside the cockpit and are controlled from the cockpit using your foot pedals. By pushing forward on your right foot pedal, you'll cause your boat to turn to the right; push on the left and you'll turn to the left. Besides helping you to keep your boat on course when paddling in wind or current and helping to turn your kayak in tight places, one of the great advantages to having a rudder is that it allows you to control the angle of your kayak with your feet during a downwind drift. This leaves your hands free to do what you're there for… to catch fish!

Skegs are stored in a skeg box that is embedded in the stern of the kayak and they are deployed by use of a slider found alongside the cockpit. Because skegs don't swivel side to side, their control comes from the depth at which they are set. The more your kayak wants to weathercock, the deeper you'll set the skeg. Since skegs are only really useful for tracking over long distances, you generally don't find them on recreational or fishing kayaks.

CHOOSING A KAYAK FISHING LOCATION

If the quick trips after work are like a snack, then the all-day trips on the weekends are the full course meal. And planning for those trips is half the fun. Make sure that you watch the weather reports so that you know what type of conditions you'll be dealing with, but remember that kayaks allow you the option of launching from places where boaters can't. Take advantage of this asset and you can usually find a protected area to fish even on the windiest of days. Anywhere you can park your vehicle and access the water without trespassing is fair game. Bridges over creeks or rivers are perfect launch points, as are roadside parks. Given the light weight and durability of today's fishing kayaks, it isn't too difficult to negotiate moderately rough terrain in your quest for under-utilized waters. We've launched our kayaks from a variety of locations that many people would never even consider.

You probably already have a couple of places in mind for your area, but once you get into the sport you'll likely find yourself looking at things a bit differently. Many of our favorite fishing holes were discovered while driving around the countryside. Any time we cross a body of water that appears big enough to accommodate a kayak, we make note of it for further investigation. From there it is simply a matter of using the Internet to search out maps and aerial photos to find out whether or not this piece of water looks interesting enough to warrant an investigatory trip. It isn't exactly pioneering the West, but it does give a sense of exploration.

Of course this is all dependent upon what type of water we're talking about. If it is a piece of flat water, perhaps the arm of a bay estuary or a lake, then the exploration is rather simple. You can drop in and paddle in either direction and be relatively secure in knowing that you can safely explore the area and return to your launch. Moving water will require a bit more planning and preparation. You'll need to learn to judge the flow rate and do a bit more background research on the waterway. Local river guide books can be invaluable in determining whether or not the waterway is within your skill level. On lesser creeks you'll need to check the topographical maps to learn whether there might be potential dangers downstream. You'll also need to plan on setting up a shuttle if the flow is too great to paddle back upstream to your launch.

Overnight camping trips are also a viable option for the kayak angler. The storage capacity of today's fishing kayaks allows you to take along plenty of gear for a multi-day trip. Camping gear designed for backpackers is perfect for the kayak camper. Small compact tents, sleeping bags and even cooking supplies are readily available. This opens up a whole world of fishing possibilities that are unreachable on a day trip. In our modern world of convenience stores and fast food, there is something very satisfying about paddling to a distant shoreline to set up camp and then going out to catch your own dinner.

The best kayak launches are sloping beaches where you can pull your kayak out onto the water, then straddle it and hop in.

CRAB MAN
yak Launch
and
Parking Fee
$2.00 per unit *Mgr.*

CHOOSING A GOOD LAUNCH

Once you've decided where you're going for the day, it's important to pick a good spot to launch. The closer you can get to the water the better. Even the lightest kayak weighs a good bit and you're better off saving your energy for fishing. A good launch site isn't all about being right on the water though. You want to choose a spot where your vehicle is well off the road and in a safe area. Consider also the landmarks near your vehicle. After a long day out on any large body of water when the wind has picked up and your energy levels have gone down, a billboard or water tower will provide a great target to guide you back to your vehicle.

Forward Stroke

Reverse Stroke

Sweep Strokes

Draw Strokes

Re-entering Your Kayak
From the Water

THE ESSENTIAL STROKES AND SAFETY

chapter three

Most of the people who get into kayak fishing are either anglers looking for a new experience and a way to catch the big one, or paddlers looking to add a new dimension to their sport. Either way, proper paddling technique is important to learn because it will allow you to stay out on the water longer, increase the area you can comfortably fish on a given day and help you to avoid overuse injuries. Simply put, developing good paddling technique will enhance your kayak fishing experience.

FORWARD STROKE

Although any stroke that gets your kayak moving forward is fine, with a proper forward stroke, you'll be able to get where you want to go more efficiently and with the least amount of wasted effort. The bottom line is that you'll give yourself more fishing time!

Since the forward stroke is the stroke that you'll use 99% of the time, we're going to look at it in a fair amount of depth. In fact, we're going to look at the stroke in three distinct parts: catch, rotation, and recovery.

CATCH

The catch refers to the moment when your paddle blade is planted in the water. Sitting up straight, with a relaxed grip on your paddle, reach to your toes and plant your blade fully into the water. This reaching action involves both your arms and your shoulders. Do not lean forward at the waist to reach to your toes, but rather twist from the waist. If you're reaching for a stroke with your right blade, you'll push your right shoulder forward while reaching with your right arm. This shoulder-reach causes you to rotate or "wind-up" your upper torso and is commonly referred to as torso rotation. Torso

To plant your forward stroke, reach with the blade toward your toes by twisting at the waist.

Make sure that as you pull on your stroke, the blade is fully submerged.

When the paddle blade reaches your hip, the forward stroke is done, and you can slice your paddle up out of the water.

1

2

3

rotation lets you harness the power of your front and side stomach muscles for your strokes rather than just using your arms. With your body wound up, spear your blade into the water so that the whole blade is submerged. Once that blade is completely in the water, you'll then pull on your paddle and unwind your upper body to drive your boat forward.

One of the most common mistakes is pulling on the forward stroke before the blade is fully submerged in the water. If you're doing this, you'll notice your strokes creating a lot of splash, which means that you're actually wasting energy pulling water past your kayak rather than pulling your kayak forward through the water. To understand this better, imagine that you're planting your paddle in cement when you take a stroke, and then pulling yourself up to the paddle, rather than pulling the paddle back to yourself. The only way this will work is if you have fully and securely planted your whole blade in the water.

ROTATION

Once it's wound up, your body is like an elastic band in that you'll have a lot of potential energy at your command. Rotation refers to the way you'll use this energy to power your forward stroke.

As described above, after the catch, your body should be wound up and your paddle firmly planted at your toes. You'll now pull on your paddle and drive your kayak forward using as much of your large torso muscles as possible rather than relying on your comparatively weak arms to do the work. In fact, a good way to think about this is that your arms are just a supplement to the power of your torso. True power comes from your stomach, side and back muscles. If you don't believe it, try paddling forward with your arms locked straight at the elbows. Paddling in this manner may seem awkward at first, but you can really get your boat moving—and the only way to do it is with pronounced torso rotation.

As soon as one stroke finishes, drop the opposite blade into the water at the toes.

Notice that the arms move very little as the stroke is pulled through. The power for the stroke comes from torso rotation.

By minimizing the movement of your kayak while you paddle forward, it will glide more efficiently through the water, and most importantly, help you avoid startling fish.

Notice the active blade is fully submerged and the top hand is at around chin level.

Now that you're engaging the most powerful muscles, let's take a quick look at what the rest of your body will be doing. With elbows bent and staying low, pull on the paddle with your arms as you take each stroke. Since your torso will be doing the bulk of the work, the motion of your arms will be quite small. As a general rule, the more vertical the paddle shaft is while taking a forward stroke, the more power you're getting from it. To get the paddle more vertical, bring your top hand higher and further across your boat. These sprinting strokes are great when you're in a hurry, but they're also very tiring. For general paddling purposes, keep your top hand at about shoulder or chest level. In very shallow water you'll find that you need to lower your top hand a bit and allow the blade to maintain a shallower angle with less of the blade entering the water.

For maximum drive, your legs can also be involved with your forward stroke. By pushing with the foot on the same side that you're taking a stroke you will help transfer more power to your stroke.

RECOVERY

The recovery is the point at which your forward stroke ends and the blade gets removed from the water. This happens at your hip, which is earlier than most paddlers expect or practice. When your stroke reaches your hip, slice your paddle up out of the water sideways and get ready for the next stroke, which means unwinding your body past its position of rest and then winding it up in the opposite direction, ready for the next catch of your other blade on the other side.

Now that you have all the pieces for an efficient and powerful forward stroke, try to put them all together as smoothly as possible while keeping your boat as "quiet" as you can. A "quiet" boat has minimal bob from side to side or up and down, and will glide through the water most efficiently.

REVERSE STROKE

Although you might not use the reverse stroke very often, it can come in handy when maneuvering to set up for a cast and in narrow channels.

Not surprisingly, the reverse stroke is just like the forward stroke, only done in reverse. The first thing to know is that you shouldn't rotate the paddle in your hands to use the power face. Your grip on the shaft will remain the same as always, which means you'll use the backside of the paddle for the stroke.

With your top hand held in a relaxed position in front of your body at a level between chest and chin height, plant your blade just behind your hip and push it to your toes. As you plant your blade deeply in the water behind your hip, turn your upper body in the same direction. By rotating towards your paddle like this you can use the power of torso rotation as you did with your forward stroke. After your stroke reaches your toes, wind your body up in the other direction to get ready to drop the next stroke behind your hip on the opposite side.

As a final note, remember to look behind you every few strokes to avoid running into something or someone else! It's easiest to do this by glancing behind you as you plant your stroke.

USING THE REVERSE STROKE AS A BRAKE

Whether you are approaching a dock, a boat, or paddling over to your buddy to get one of the lures that seems to be working a lot better for him than the ones you have, you're going to need to put on the brakes at some point. You'll do so with a series of short and quick alternating reverse strokes called "braking" strokes. With three short and powerful braking strokes, you should be able to fully stop your kayak from any speed.

1

The back stroke is planted firmly in the water, just behind your hip and with your upper body rotated towards it.

2

Notice the arms stay in a relatively fixed position. Torso rotation provides much of the power for the stroke.

3

The reverse stroke finishes when your blade reaches your toes.

4

Wind up your body in the other direction before planting the next blade.

5

Plant the paddle fully in the water before pushing on it.

6

Once again, torso rotation provides the real power for your reverse stroke.

SWEEP STROKES

Most fishing kayaks are designed to travel well in a straight line and not designed to turn very much. This means that it will take a few good strokes to turn a fishing kayak around. Sweep strokes are what you're going to use. You can use forward and/or reverse sweep strokes while stationary or when moving. We're going to take a quick look at the technique used for both.

FORWARD SWEEP

The forward sweep stroke is usually used to turn a kayak while stationary or to make small course corrections while traveling forward.

Just like the forward stroke, the forward sweep starts with your body wound up and your blade completely in the water at your toes. It also harnesses the power of torso rotation. Unlike the forward stroke, your hands will stay very low during the sweep and your blade will follow an arcing path as far out to the side of your kayak as possible. To do this, the hand controlling the active blade will reach out over the water while the other maintains a low position in front of your stomach. Your blade will continue on its arcing path until it approaches the stern of your boat. You'll then slice your paddle out of the water before it touches the stern and move to your next stroke.

When you practice this stroke, keep your eyes on the active blade throughout its arc to get the most power from your torso rotation. Following the blade with your eyes will force your upper body to rotate throughout the stroke. Once you've become very comfortable with the forward sweep, you'll be able keep your eyes on where you're going instead of following the blade. You can also push off the foot pedal on the sweeping-stroke side of the boat for even more power.

REVERSE SWEEP

The reverse sweep is simply a forward sweep done in reverse—and like the reverse stroke, you'll use the backside of your paddle. The reverse sweep is an effective tool for the kayak angler as well. Have you ever been slowly cruising a shoreline only to see some activity peripherally just behind you? A good reverse sweep on the shoreline side of your boat will stop your forward movement and turn you quickly into position to cast at your prey.

The reverse sweep starts with your body wound up and your blade completely in the water at the stern of your kayak about six inches away from the hull. In order to put the most torso rotation possible into your stroke, keep your eyes on the active paddle blade. With the blade planted deeply in the water, sweep a wide arc all the way out to the side of your kayak up to your toes. The hand on the side of the active blade reaches out over the water while the other stays in front of your stomach. By keeping your head turning with your active blade, you will encourage good torso rotation and ensure that your body unwinds throughout the whole stroke.

> **TIP:**
>
> Once you're comfortable with both sweep strokes, try combining the two. A forward sweep on one side followed by a reverse sweep on the opposite side is the quickest way to turn a stationary kayak.

The forward sweep starts with your body wound up and your paddle planted deeply at your toes with the shaft held low.

Keeping your hands low, sweep an arcing path far out to the side of the kayak.

The reverse sweep starts at the stern of your kayak with your head and body aggressively rotated towards it.

Keeping your hands low, sweep a wide arc with your paddle.

Follow your active blade with your eyes to help incorporate torso rotation into the stroke.

Finish your sweep before your paddle hits the stern of your kayak.

Notice the arms have stayed in a relatively fixed position throughout the stroke, which means torso rotation is providing much of the power.

The stroke ends after having swept a full, wide arc.

DRAW STROKES

Draw strokes are used to move your kayak sideways, such as when you want to pull yourself up beside a buddy, a boat, or a dock.

BASIC DRAW

The basic draw involves reaching out to the side of your kayak at the hip and pulling water towards you. For the most effective stroke, plant your blade completely in the water, rotate your head and upper body to face your active blade, and hold your paddle as vertical as possible. Getting your paddle vertical requires reaching across your upper body with your top hand. This takes some real balance so you might want to start by practicing your draw stroke with your top hand held lower and in front of your face. With your blade planted fully in the water, your top hand will stay quite stationary, acting as a pivot point for the stroke while you pull your lower hand in towards your hip. Now, before your paddle blade hits your kayak, you need to finish the stroke by slicing the blade out of the water towards the stern. This should happen when your blade is about six inches away from the side of your kayak. If you bring your blade in too close, it can accidentally get pinned against the side of your boat and throw you off balance.

T-STROKE DRAW

When you get comfortable with the basic draw, you can try the T-stroke. The only difference between the T-stroke and the basic draw is that instead of slicing the blade out of the water towards the stern at the end of the stroke, you'll curl your wrists forward to turn the blade perpendicular to your boat and then slice it back out to where it started. Now you are set up to repeat the draw. This can be a very smooth and efficient way to move sideways.

The draw stroke is a great way to pull up alongside a dock. Reach out to the side of the kayak and then pull the blade toward your hip using the power face of your paddle.

1

The T-stroke is initiated the same way as the basic draw—with your head and upper body turned to face the active paddle blade.

2

Instead of slicing your paddle out of the water at the end of the draw, curl your wrists forward to turn the blade 90 degrees.

3

Slice your paddle back out to where it started.

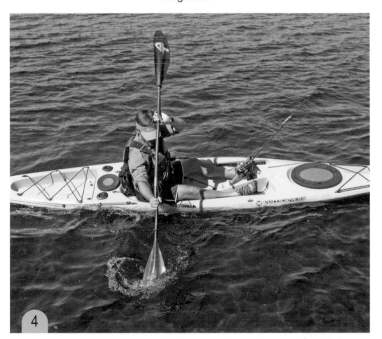

4

Turn your wrists again and you're in position for another draw stroke.

If you find your boat turning as you take either a basic draw or T-stroke, it means that you're doing your draw too far forward or too far back. If your draw is too far forward, you'll pull your bow towards your paddle and your boat will turn. If your draw is too far back, you'll be pulling your stern towards your paddle.

SCULLING DRAW

An even more advanced technique for drawing your kayak sideways is called the sculling draw. Although it's more powerful than the other two draw strokes, it requires more paddle dexterity. It is a great stroke to learn once you're proficient with the other draw strokes. The sculling draw is set up in the same way as the T-stroke. Reaching out to the side of your hip, place your blade completely in the water with your head and upper body rotated aggressively to face it. Push

your top hand across your boat to get your paddle as vertical as possible. Instead of pulling directly into your hip though, you'll use something we call a sculling motion. You now pull steadily on your paddle without having the blade draw closer to the side of your kayak. This removes the recovery phase that the other draw strokes require.

The key to sculling is keeping your paddle blade moving along a short path forward and backward about a foot or two out to the side of your kayak with a blade angle that opens your power face to the oncoming water and pulls your paddle away from your kayak. This unique blade angle is commonly referred to as a "climbing angle". Climbing angle means that the leading edge of your paddle blade is higher than the trailing edge. It uses the same motion that you unconsciously use when buttering bread. The leading edge has to stay higher than the trailing edge or else you're cutting into the bread. When you're learning the sculling draw, it can actually be a useful thing to

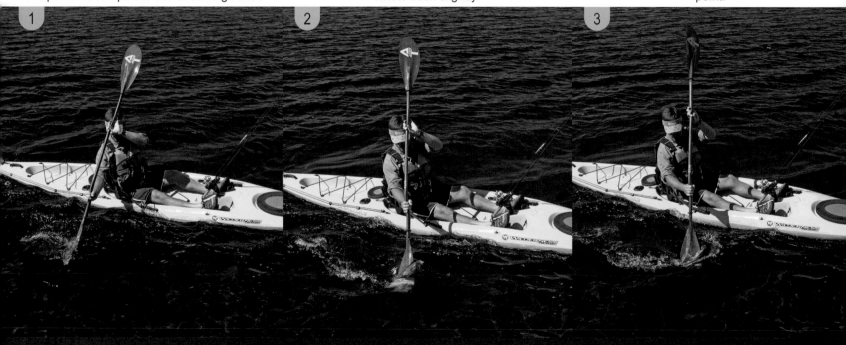

Sculling involves moving your paddle blade along a short path alongside your kayak with the power face open to the oncoming water.

As you slice your blade forward, cock your wrists back slightly.

Notice the top hand acts much like a pivot point.

1

2

3

visualize evenly spreading something thick like peanut butter on toast. To maintain a climbing angle on your blade while performing the sculling draw you'll cock your wrists slightly back as you slice your blade forward. You then make a quick transition and curl your wrists slightly forward as you slice your blade backward. Keep in mind that the change in blade angle is subtle. If you open your power face too much, you'll be pushing your kayak forward and backward rather than drawing it sideways.

Using this sculling technique, you can apply steady drawing pressure with your paddle blade and move your boat sideways at a surprising speed. Don't forget that just like any other stroke, the power for your sculling draw comes from your torso rotation. This is why it's so important that you turn your body aggressively into the stroke. The forward and backward movement of your paddle can then be driven by your torso rotation, while your arms will stay in a relatively fixed position.

RE-ENTERING YOUR KAYAK FROM THE WATER

Although kayaks are very stable, it's common sense to be prepared for the unlikely situation that requires you to re-enter your kayak from the water. One of the huge advantages of sit-on-top kayaks is that they are so easy to get back into from the water. Divers have used these types of boats for years for the simple reason that they can easily hop into the water and make a dive from them. When the dive is over they can throw their tank and gear back on top and climb aboard. Sit-inside kayaks simply don't provide this flexibility—but with a little practice and some help from a friend, you can learn to quickly and reliably re-enter a sit-inside. The problem remaining is that since sit-insides aren't self-bailing, you'll have a lot of water to pump out of your kayak once you're back in the seat.

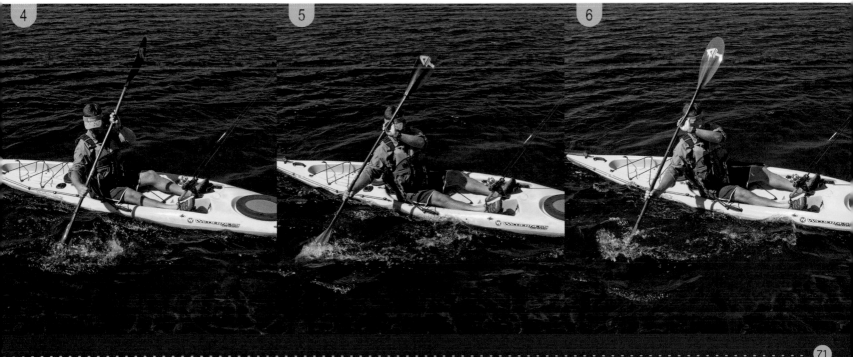

As you pull towards the stern, curl your wrists forward slightly.

With your hands held in relatively fixed positions, your torso rotation will provide much of the power for the stroke.

Throughout the sculling draw, the active blade remains one-and-a-half or two feet away from the side of your kayak.

To get back into a sit-on-top, approach the kayak from side and get your feet on the surface of the water behind you. Then, with a kick of the legs and push up with the arms, draw your body on top of the kayak, keeping your weight low.

The most important thing in having the confidence to re-enter either style of kayak is practice, practice, practice! Do not just do it once and think you've got it figured out. Start off on flat, calm water and get your technique down. Once you get comfortable with your abilities, move to some rougher water and try again. We suggest this because it is much more likely that should you be faced with this situation in the real world, it won't be in calm conditions. If you live near the coast, the surf is the perfect place to test yourself. Always wear your PFD and have at least one buddy with you while practicing.

RE-ENTERING A SIT-ON-TOP

If you fish from a sit-on-top kayak for long, there's a reasonable chance that you'll find yourself taking an unscheduled swim and needing to get back on top of your kayak from the water. Hopefully your kayak didn't actually flip over, and if it did, any equipment that wasn't stored inside was tied down. If it

did flip upside-down, you can right your boat by approaching it from the side and scrambling over the hull to grab the far edge. In this position, you will have the leverage necessary to right the kayak by pulling it towards you. Pushing up on the near side is much more difficult. When practicing, try both methods to get a better understanding of what we're talking about.

Once the kayak is right-side-up, getting back in is a fairly simple process, but it does require a small amount of explosive power. Start by positioning yourself alongside the kayak by the seat. You can keep your paddle in one hand, slide it under your deck lines so that it doesn't get away from you, or give it to your paddling buddy. With a firm grip on the kayak, let your legs float to the surface behind you. You'll then give a powerful kick with your legs and push with your arms to haul your chest up onto the kayak. Once you're up on the boat, twist your body around and settle into the seat. You can then swing your legs back onto the boat. The whole process may not look pretty, but it works!

With the hard part accomplished, you can spin and drop your butt into the seat, and then pull your legs in.

RE-ENTERING A SIT-INSIDE

A sit-inside kayak presents a different set of problems. It holds water and will be unstable while you climb on top of it right up until the point that you are settled back into the cockpit. For these reasons, re-entering a sit-inside kayak is much easier with the help of another paddler.

If you've found yourself swimming from a sit-inside, chances are very good that your boat is upside-down. The first order of business is to flip your boat upright. When your boat is upside-down, air gets trapped inside. The trapped air keeps water from flooding the interior. This means that the quicker you can flip the boat upright, the less water will get scooped inside. Although you can flip the kayak upright yourself from the water, it is easier if your paddling buddy helps by lifting an end as you roll the kayak. With the kayak upright, your paddling partner can then stabilize the kayak as you get back in. A partner can actually provide an incredible amount of stability, although it requires a lot of commitment on his or her part. To assist, your partner positions their kayak parallel to yours and gets a good grip on the empty kayak with both hands, then leans his whole body over onto it. As long as he has a good grip on the kayak, there's virtually no chance of his flipping himself as the two "rafted" kayaks will be extremely stable. You can then use virtually the same re-entry technique as the one we just outlined for getting back into the sit-on-top kayak. You need to remember that your center of gravity will be high and this will make your kayak unstable until you've got your butt back in the seat.

Of course, once you're back inside, you'll have a fair amount of water in the boat to deal with. This is where a bilge pump comes in handy. Be sure to keep your pump stored in such a manner that it is easily accessed, but also secure enough that it doesn't float away during the capsizing. Although a bilge pump is a great piece of safety gear for any sit-inside kayak, it's a good idea to make a practice of staying close enough to shore so that you can easily head to dry land and empty your boat there.

1

The swimmer will use the same re-entry technique for a sit-inside as was just demonstrated for the sit-on-top, except they'll need the help of a friend to support their kayak.

2

The rescuer gets a firm grip on the bow and leans their weight onto the empty boat to stabilize it while the swimmer re-enters.

3

Once the swimmer has pulled themselves on top of the kayak, they'll spin and drop their butt into the seat.

4

The rescuer needs to maintain their support of the swimmer's kayak throughout the re-entry.

A hand-held bilge pump is an important piece of gear to have
if you're paddling a sit-inside kayak.

Trolling

Drift Fishing

Side-Saddle Fishing

Poling

Wade Fishing from a
Kayak

Fly Fishing

Using Bait

Using Lures

Fishing from a Tandem

Fishing with Kids

Using a Power Boat as a
Mothership

On-the-Water Safety

FISHING FROM A KAYAK

chapter four

4

Now that you have all the equipment you need, have chosen your fishing location, and have learned how to paddle your kayak, it is time to figure out the best method for catching those fish. Assuming that you already have a basic idea of how to fish, it is just a matter of adapting your fishing style to the kayak. Fishing methods vary greatly throughout the country depending on the locale, conditions and the species being sought. It would be quite presumptuous, not to mention unbelievable, for us to pretend that we could cover every situation encountered by anglers everywhere. Just thumbing through the national fishing supply catalogues can leave you scratching your head trying to figure out what some of these contraptions are used for. Even with all the varied methods and species, there aren't too many fishing situations that can't be handled from a kayak.

TROLLING

Trolling from a power boat is a very effective way of catching fish. The same is true from a kayak. Some people choose to drift with the current or wind while dragging a lure or bait. Others choose to propel themselves at a steady pace with their paddle. Both styles have one thing in common: the most successful anglers don't simply drift along or paddle without purpose—they will concentrate their efforts by passing over or near some sort of structure. This is a much higher percentage method than aimlessly covering water. The type of structure targeted depends on the type of fish you are seeking. As stated earlier, it is assumed that you have a basic understanding of the fish you want to target in your area. Use that knowledge and the kayak to your advantage.

Perhaps one of the most exciting methods of kayak trolling is to target actively feeding schools of fish on the surface. Predators blitzing baitfish often draw gulls or other birds to the fray. Watch for a tight group of birds hovering and diving into the water. This is your flashing neon sign. Once you figure out which way the school is headed, you can set yourself up to intercept them. Try to pass in front of the school and time it so that your trailing lure passes through the leading edge of the school. The most aggressively feeding fish will usually be at the front of the pack. This is where the kayak really shines. A kayaker can pass much closer to the activity than a power boat without spooking the fish. On a recent trip we made numerous passes straight through the middle of the melee. The fish were moving so fast that it was nearly impossible not to do so, but it didn't seem to have any affect on the feeding frenzy. We probably couldn't have gotten away with running a power boat through them.

Some kayak anglers prefer trolling with two or more rigs, but we feel this invites catastrophe. With actively feeding fish, the chances of hooking more than one fish are fairly high, and this is not the most desirable situation when you're alone in a small craft. Dealing with one bent rod while stowing the paddle and trying to keep everything under control is hard enough. Multiply the number of hooked fish and you'll quickly learn the meaning of chaos.

For this type of fishing it is essential to have a good quality rod holder that is securely attached to the kayak. A large fish hitting a lure full force will surely test your equipment. Riveted rod holders can sometimes be ripped loose in these situations. Do yourself a favor and attach them to your kayak with bolts, washers, and nuts—and as an added precaution, it would be wise to invest in a rod leash of some type. As stated above, this is an exciting type of fishing. Many things can happen all at once and it only takes a minimal lapse in concentration to lose a rod while trying to secure your paddle and retrieve your rig from the holder.

DRIFT FISHING

Drift fishing is our common method for covering water. Fishing the coast often means dealing with the wind so you may as well work with it instead of trying to fight it. The term "drift fishing" sounds as though you are aimlessly floating with wind or current, but when done correctly it is a high percentage method of searching for fish. This is where a rudder comes into play. Predator fish are fond of using structure to search out or ambush their prey. Structure can mean many things. It can mean,

of course, hard material objects like rocks, logs, or reefs; but it can also refer to less obvious things, like a spot where water clarity changes. Set yourself up in a position that allows you to drift in the general direction of the structure you intend to target. Now put away your paddle and use the rudder to steer yourself into position while you cast. Depending on the wind speed, the rudder will allow you to move 30 to 45 degrees to the right or left. If you've set yourself up in a target-rich environment, you will be able to work a long stretch of water without ever having to pick up your paddle. We've used this method alongside other anglers who don't have rudders and watched as they constantly alternated between their paddle and rod. We can say for certain that having a rudder in play will dramatically increase the number of quality casts you can make in a day.

This method of controlled drifting is quite versatile. It can be employed for working your way in and out along an irregular shoreline. It works great for covering the sandy potholes of an open grass flat. And it is deadly effective for working your way down a creek and hitting every point, gravel bar, or deep pool.

Small drift anchors may also be employed in a situation

When fishing side-saddle, you're usually best off turning so that your casting arm is on the bow side of your kayak—this way any gear in the stern won't get in your way.

where the wind is pushing you too fast. The drift anchor acts as a parachute to slow your drift and allow you to more thoroughly fish an area. You can also vary the point of attachment on your kayak to control the angle of your craft during the drift. We generally secure the drift anchor to the area just behind and to the right of the seat. This positions the kayak to drift at a slight angle and allows you to comfortably cast downwind without fear of striking the rods stowed behind your seat. In the absence of a drift anchor, sitting side-saddle with your legs in the water will also slow your drift if you have a sit-on-top kayak.

SIDE-SADDLE FISHING

Side-saddle is a very popular method for fishing from a sit-on-top kayak. While it can be used to drift fish through deeper areas, this method really shines in shallow water where you can touch the bottom. Depending on the model of kayak you own, there is usually one spot in the cockpit that is most comfortable for sitting side-saddle. Something to note is that rounded edges are easy on the legs, so when checking out kayaks you may want to test them to see how comfortable they are when sitting side-saddle.

The best way to position yourself is with your casting arm towards the bow. With all of your gear stored towards the rear of the kayak, this will give you an unobstructed cast. Because you don't have to worry about hitting anything, you can concentrate on the fishing. Another advantage to sitting this way in shallow water is that you can control your kayak without using your paddle. Simply walk your feet across the bottom and stop where you like. This method allows you to thoroughly work an area and to fish in places where the bottom is too muddy for wading. With most of your weight being supported by the kayak, you won't sink deep into the soft bottom.

POLING

Poling is not a terribly popular method of kayak fishing for obvious reasons. Standing up in a kayak takes a combination of a very stable craft, calm waters and an excellent sense of balance. The Wilderness Systems Ride is an example of a kayak that is conducive to standing up because it is unbelievably stable. Some anglers prefer to use a push pole designed specifically for poling in addition to their paddle. We have found that it is easier and nearly as effective to just use the paddle for poling. The practical application of poling in a kayak is somewhat limited. Standing up allows you to see down into the water for sight-casting to cruising or bedded fish. As such, it is really only useful in areas with clear shallow water, light winds, and little current. But when the conditions are right it can be extremely effective. Having the ability to spot a fish and make a good presentation definitely increases the odds in your favor.

We were hesitant to even include this section because not many people can safely stand up in a kayak and even fewer feel secure enough to stand and fish. Should you decide to give this a try, get yourself a sit-on-top kayak with high initial stability like the Ride. A sit-inside kayak is not really designed for standing and fishing. While it can certainly be done in certain models of sit-insides, it makes a lot more sense from a sit-on top. Take the kayak out to an area with a level sandy bottom and leave all your gear in your vehicle. Chances are high that you won't get the hang of it right

Fishing kayaks are so stable that in many conditions it's possible to fish from a standing position, which gives you a better view.

away, so you should be prepared to get wet. To practice, carefully get up onto your knees and stay there until you feel secure with your balance. Next try standing up slowly. If you feel off balance, just stand still. Do not try to compensate by leaning the other way. If you are in a truly stable kayak, it will right itself and settle down quickly. If you are still feeling off-balance, simply step out. It is much easier on your ego than falling out. And whatever you do, don't look straight up at a passing bird. (This is experience talking.) Finally, please do not try this in dangerous conditions like high wind or strong currents and avoid trying to stand in your boat over a bottom that could cause injury should you fall out.

WADE FISHING FROM A KAYAK

We often use our kayaks to access secluded flats and then get out. There are some situations where it just makes more sense to wade. Always use your paddle to check the depth of water and the firmness of the bottom. It is quite embarrassing and sometimes dangerous to just hop out expecting a firm bottom and shallow water only to find yourself literally in over your head. You have the option of simply anchoring your kayak and walking away or you can try our preferred method. What we like to do is tie ourselves to the kayak via a bow line. This way you are bringing your trusty steed along with you and it's at the ready if the need arises to quickly relocate. A downside to tying yourself to the boat is that you have little control over where the kayak floats as you wade. It can get pretty frustrating to be wading along with the wind at your back and have the kayak getting in your way as it floats past you. A simple fix for this problem is to drop some sort of weight off the stern of your kayak and allow the weight to drag on a short rope along the bottom. We've used everything from large fishing weights to anchors tied backwards. Anything that will not actually catch on the bottom will work.

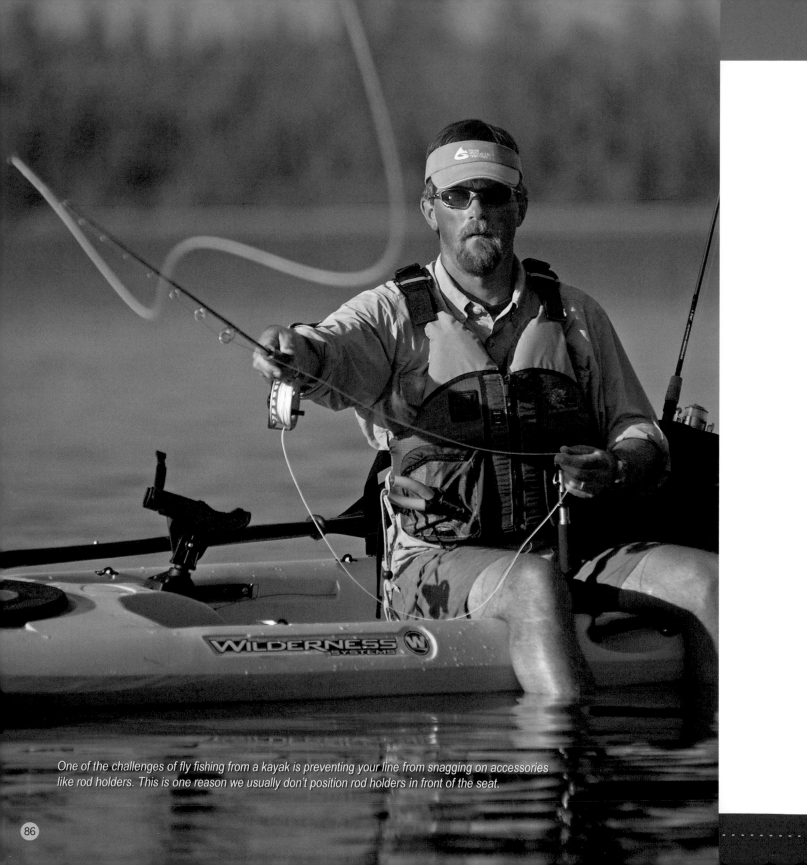

One of the challenges of fly fishing from a kayak is preventing your line from snagging on accessories like rod holders. This is one reason we usually don't position rod holders in front of the seat.

Fly Fishing

Many people who fly fish are being drawn to the kayak as a mode of transportation to get them to their favorite fishing destinations. Often times it only takes a short paddle trip to get you away from the drive-up wading crowd. Whether you are fishing fresh or salt, the difference between success and getting skunked can be as simple as moving a few hundred yards from where the crowd has been pounding the water. While the kayak is a fine mode of transportation for reaching your wading grounds, it can also be a very useful fly fishing platform.

A sit-inside kayak provides the angler with a perfect place to store the stripped fly line. The front deck can be left clear of obstructions or a mini spray skirt can be installed to facilitate shooting the fly line with minimal chance of snagging. Knowing that fly line has a mind of its own and can often hang up on the most insignificant thing, it is important to carefully check for any possible snags while rigging your kayak. If you intend to fly fish from your kayak, avoid mounting any accessories that could interfere with the storage of your excess line. A flat open area is essential to keeping everything moving smoothly.

The sit-on-top kayak presents its own special set of problems for fly fishing, but also has some distinct advantages. On the downside there isn't a flat open space for your line. Fly line stripped into your lap and across your legs is just begging to hang up on something. Foot pegs, wading boots and paddle holders are all common line-grabbing culprits. In Texas, most of our saltwater fly fishing is for redfish in very shallow water. It is a different kind of fishing where we often spend a considerable

Although live bait is one of the most effective ways to catch fish, keeping live bait alive while kayak fishing is a challenge.

amount of time searching out a single feeding fish in a few inches of water. These are easily-spooked creatures that will often only allow a single presentation. Nothing is more frustrating than finally getting in position for the shot only to have it fall a few feet short of the target because the fly line snagged on a boot lace. Well, there is something more frustrating. Getting that same fish to eat your fly and then pull free when the fly line inexplicably wraps itself around the water bottle you left lying in the cockpit. Just be aware that if there is anything that could possibly tangle your fly line, it will—and it will invariably happen at the worst possible moment. To avoid the frustration we often sit side-saddle towards the center of the cockpit and strip excess line into the seat area, which has smooth contours and works really well as a stripping basket.

USING BAIT

If you were to take a survey of anglers you'd probably find that the most popular way to fish is with some kind of bait. Bait can be anything from live species of prey to a store-bought concoction that smells so bad you don't want to touch it without wearing gloves. We're lure-chuckers at heart, but over the years we've baited many a hook with everything from foot-long mullet to tiny shrimp to stinking catfish dough bait and even whole kernel corn. Obviously there is very little extra preparation needed to use dead or inanimate bait from the kayak. Simply bring your usual gear, stow your bait where it is easily accessible and go fishing.

Live bait is probably one of the most effective ways to catch fish. Put a hook in what the game fish naturally eat and you stand a pretty good chance of feeding some fish. The lure manufacturers are coming close, but they still can't completely reproduce Mother Nature's handiwork. The challenge with using live bait from a kayak is storing the bait and keeping it alive. Some types of live bait are simple and don't require much thought. A bucket of worms or a can of crickets can be brought along easily. Baitfish require more planning. You'll need some sort of holding tank and fresh oxygenated water. In some cases this can be accomplished with a floating bait bucket towed alongside the kayak. This works fine in situations where paddling distances aren't an issue.

When dragging a bait bucket is out of the question, there are several other methods to consider. A bucket, small ice chest, or other type of container can be placed in the tankwell while battery operated aerators or recirculating pumps keep the baitfish inside the container alive. Several bait tanks designed specifically for use in kayaks are now on the market. Keep in mind that water is heavy and storing it in or on your kayak will change the way the kayak handles. A large amount of sloshing water could jeopardize the stability of the kayak. Use the smallest tank possible for the application. Also try using one of the gel cell batteries to power the pump. These batteries are rechargeable, relatively small and lightweight, and they will power a small pump all day. You will also need to consider how easily you can reach your bait from the seated position. Do yourself a favor and spend some time sitting in the kayak in the yard testing your bait placement prior to heading out on

the water. Perhaps the best method when using larger bait fish is to catch them as needed while on the water. This isn't always practical, but it is very handy when the bait fish are present on the fishing grounds.

USING LURES

The biggest challenge for the lure fanatic is often in minimizing the amount of gear. For the power boater transitioning to the kayak, this can sometimes be a real test. We all know the guy who brings along a tackle box that could double as a suitcase. If you are that guy, try to pare down your lure selection to what you actually think you'll be using. Wade and bank anglers are generally accustomed to packing light and will have no problem transitioning to the kayak. In fact, with a kayak they'll be free to pack more gear than they would normally carry. We prefer to have one small box with a reasonable variety of lures stored

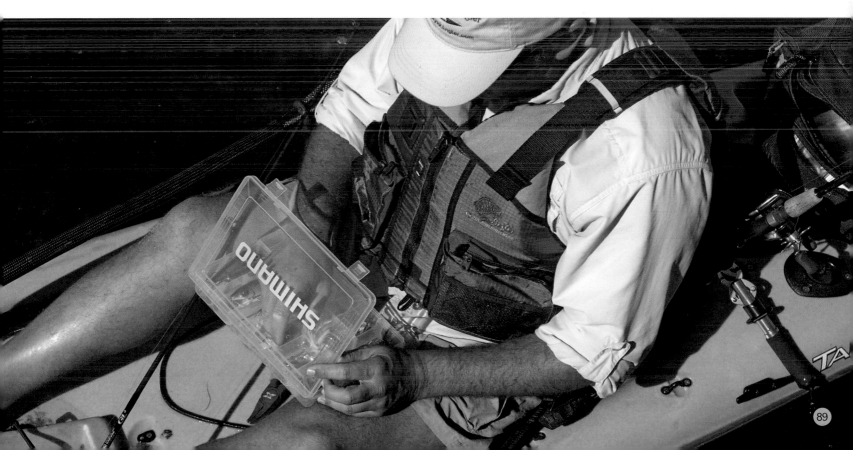

within easy reach. Additional boxes with back-up lures can be stowed inside the hatches just in case you run low on the hot bait. Of course, stowing gear in hatches assumes you'll be fishing in an area where you can pull into shallow water or even to shore so that you can step out of the kayak to retrieve your cache. If you are fishing in deep open water then you need to have everything already within reach. Try to keep it as simple as possible. Within a few trips you'll have your own system set up.

FISHING FROM A TANDEM

"Can we fish from that tandem?" We get this question all the time. The answer is yes, but it isn't a great idea. The math just doesn't work. Two people in a 13 to 15-foot kayak, each armed with a 6-foot rod and a lure with multiple treble hooks just adds up to trouble. The question usually comes from a couple and the wife has veto power on the purchase. She's willing to go out fishing, but she's not so sure about paddling to get there. After a few minutes of explaining just how easy it is to paddle a kayak and perhaps getting her on the water for a demo, the deal is sealed. They're getting his and hers kayaks.

Even for people who want to take their kids with them, I'll usually suggest getting two kayaks instead of a tandem. With a little patience and instruction, even very young kids are perfectly capable of handling their own kayaks in protected waters. You'll both be happier.

The only time a tandem will work well for fishing is if one person is going to paddle while the other fishes. This is usually a parent with a very young child. There are also guides out there who paddle from the rear of the kayak while their client fishes from the bow. Although some will disagree, we strongly believe tandems are better suited to pleasure paddling.

FISHING WITH KIDS

By Scott Null

Speaking of taking the kids fishing, here's my favorite part of the book. Taking the kids outside and getting them away from the television should be every parent's goal. So many young ones are living life through others these days and not getting to experience life. I understand that it isn't easy, but nothing really worthwhile ever is. I've been taking my girls out fishing and hunting since they were just big enough to walk. In fact, I think one of them was out on a boat when she was still just crawling. Your kids are probably tougher and more resilient than you give them credit for. I know mine have constantly surprised me with what they'll put up with to be outdoors. I'm not suggesting you should push them through a grueling 20 mile paddle, but don't underestimate them either.

Nobody knows your kids like you do. You have a pretty good idea of their capabilities and their attention span. You also know what makes them happy and what makes them whine. Use that hard-earned knowledge to plan the day. I can't tell you exactly how to pull this off because there is a huge difference between introducing a five-year-old to fishing and trying to get your teenage daughter to spend the day with dad.

Plan for a great day, but be prepared for the worst. By that I mean: keep them happy with enough food, drinks, and snacks; keep them comfortable with the proper clothing; and make the whole excursion fun and relaxed by keeping things simple. Have your basic first aid kit stocked and ready so you can handle unexpected emergencies calmly and effectively. Be prepared to call it a day early if the fun just isn't happening. The quickest way to ruin your child on fishing and the outdoors forever is to push them too hard and make it a miserable experience. Remember that you already have an interest in fishing or else you wouldn't have read this book. However, your child's interest might need some cultivating and the key to that is making sure they have a good time.

With young children it is important to have realistic expectations. Everyone dreams of getting their child hooked up with a trophy fish. The reality is that you need to set your sights a bit lower. Think back to when you were just starting out. For little kids, anything that will stretch their line or dunk their bobber will be exciting. In fresh water this might mean putting a worm on a hook and hanging out by the docks catching perch. In the salt you can't beat shrimp on the bottom for sure-fire action—and action is what you want. Save the game fish chase for later.

With very young children, you might want to think about paddling a tandem. Put them up front where you can keep an eye on them. If they're big enough, go ahead and give them a paddle. They probably won't paddle much, but it helps make them feel like they're part of the activity. Again, don't force the issue. Provide the level of instruction and encouragement you think they can handle.

With older kids you should consider letting them paddle their own kayak. Assess their skills and make the call whenever you feel confident they can handle it. My girls were paddling on their own as early as ten years old. Those first outings were in protected water under close supervision. I also brought along a tow rope in case of a mutiny. It is amazing how quickly they'll figure it out and before long they were able to easily keep up. An unexpected bonus was when I realized that the girls were also happy and able to entertain themselves. Once they get bored with fishing they'll start searching out crabs, shrimp, and other interesting critters. They have a good time exploring sea life and I have a little more time fishing.

Equip your kids for success. Get a boat that fits them, a properly sized lightweight paddle, and a comfortable PFD. Remember: keep it simple, keep it safe, and most of all, keep it fun.

USING A POWER BOAT AS A MOTHERSHIP

Although this sport is all about the simplicity of paddling a non-motorized craft, it is not always the best way to get the job done. In certain situations it just makes sense to combine a powerboat with your kayak. You can use a small boat to

The combination of power boat and kayak provides the ultimate fishing access.

transport kayaks to distant shores where it is either impractical or unsafe to paddle to. You may also want to consider using a larger vessel as a base of operations for multi-day expeditions. Many coastal guides use their powerboats to transport kayaking clients to secluded areas that are out of reach for the average paddler. The great advantage to this strategy is that you get to fish areas that aren't often accessed.

Most often, a powerboat is used for crossing big open water and then anchored near some smaller backwater where the powerboat would be ineffective. The kayaks are then launched from the mothership and are free to go in search of fish. There are two basic ways to go about this type of trip. One is the "hit-and-run"; the other is the "base camp". If you plan ahead, you'll be able to determine which style will best suit the area you are heading to.

As the name suggests, with the hit-and-run, you'll be making multiple stops to search for productive waters. You need to keep your rigging as simple as possible to make it easy to off-load the kayaks for quick forays into the backwaters. If the chosen location proves unsuccessful, then you bring the kayaks aboard and head for new fishing grounds. Because it is usually just a short paddle back to the boat to re-supply, there is no need to bring a bunch of gear on the kayak. Fully rigging your kayak and then reversing the process several times will seriously cut into your fishing time.

The base camp method involves a bigger commitment to a chosen fishing area. For these trips you'll want to go ahead and bring all the supplies you think you'll need for a full day of fishing. If the group is planning on splitting up to cover more of the area, it is necessary to have a set time for the rendezvous back at the mothership. Your buddy's idea of "a full day of fishing" might not be the same as yours.

Another fun and effective way to make use of a powerboat is to have someone drop the group off at a distant location and then fish your way back to the original launch. This is similar to the river shuttle, but you're using a powerboat to get to your starting point. This method requires an honest assessment of how long it will take to get from point A to point B. You don't want to turn your fishing day into nothing more than a long paddle home. Give yourself plenty of time to leisurely fish your way back. Make that mistake and you'll end up disappointed that you had to bypass some prime fishing areas in order to get to the vehicle by the set time or before dark. It is also helpful to plan the trip with the prevailing wind at your back on the way in. (That's another lesson we learned the hard way.)

What about offshore fishing? There is great potential for playing on big water with kayaks. Targeting large offshore species from a kayak is a specialized game that requires a high level of skill and comes with quite a bit of risk. It is being done on a limited basis, but should only be considered if you are well-prepared and experienced with both your kayak and handling big fish. A mothership hovering close by is not a bad idea should things suddenly go south. Never fish offshore alone. There are simply too many potential hazards out on the big pond.

ON-THE-WATER SAFETY

With a little care and common sense, kayak fishing is a very safe sport that can be enjoyed by people of all ages. However, because you do it out on the water, it can get quite serious fast if things go wrong. It's for this reason that it is important that you understand and appreciate the risks and hazards involved with kayak fishing. You must assume a conservative and safety-conscious attitude when making decisions on the water.

Avoiding dangerous situations on the water is surprisingly easy. First and foremost, understand that alcohol and boating simply don't go together. Regrettably, alcohol is a major factor in nearly all boating accidents. It's also critical that you wear a PFD whenever you're on the water. By investing in a kayak fishing-specific PFD that is designed to be as comfortable and unrestricting as possible, you'll eliminate virtually any reason for wanting to remove it. They also effectively replace fishing vests. In the warmer climates where the water you'll be fishing is no more than knee deep, there's a tendency to not wear a PFD. Invariably though, an angler thinks, "Hey, maybe it'll be better over on the other side of the channel." Next thing you know, they are paddling across deep water without their lifejacket but dealing with powerboats and their wakes. Make it part of your put-in ritual. Got my lures, check, got water, check, wearing my PFD, check! It's simple and it could save your life.

On a similar note, you need to dress for the conditions. Cold water represents the biggest hazard, because being immersed in cold water can result in hypothermia very quickly. If you're paddling in cold water, you need to be even more conservative in your decisions. Paddle only in calm conditions, stay close to shore, never paddle alone and keep in mind that you're better off overdressing and being too warm than being too cold. With all that cold water around, it's easy to cool yourself off! And cooling off when you're hot is always easier than warming up when you're cold.

Another important safety issue to address is how to deal with boat traffic. It's important to know the rules of

One of the easiest ways to stay safe is to keep to water that is sheltered from wind and waves, and to always fish with a buddy.

the road—or the water. Know that when you are crossing a channel in traffic or when you are approaching an inlet, you should heed to oncoming traffic. Your biggest concern should be the powerboats and personal watercrafts that can zip around the water erratically. The best way to avoid them is to stay close to shore. It's also smart to wear brightly colored PFDs and clothing to help make you more visible. Whatever the situation, remember that you are in a kayak and just like you wouldn't bring a knife to a gunfight, don't think you can successfully challenge a power boater or expect them to back down. Use discretion and live to paddle and fish another day.

Another important safety precaution that can be taken is to use a buddy system. Avoiding kayak fishing alone raises your level of safety significantly. It can make the difference between an embarrassing episode and a life threatening experience.

DEALING WITH WEATHER

Weather will always have a bearing on whether or not you should go kayak fishing and depending on where you're paddling, you'll have different weather hazards to deal with.

In large bodies of water and on the ocean, the biggest weather concerns are wind and waves. Strong winds can push you around and make it impossible to move forward. Gusts of wind can even catch you off-guard and flip you over. Furthermore, wind can drum up waves surprisingly quickly, which only further complicates things. Avoid getting caught in nasty, windy and rough conditions. If you're going to be heading onto a big body of water, check the weather report beforehand and stay close to shore if there is any doubt regarding the conditions.

Fog can also be a serious problem. In many areas fog is quite common and can roll in quickly. The key to paddling in fog, or in areas that are subject to having fog roll in, is to hug the shoreline. You can then just turn around and follow the same shoreline back home. As a bonus, sticking close to shore pretty much guarantees you'll be out of the way of motorized boat traffic.

Rain on its own is no big deal when you're out in a kayak. In fact, paddling in the rain can be a really cool experience. But the unfortunate truth is that rain is usually accompanied by other weather. You know how to deal with wind, but what about thunder and lightning? If you hear thunder, then you know that there's lightning around, which is very dangerous to anyone out on the water. When on the water you're usually the highest point for quite a distance in any direction, making you a perfect lightning rod. At the first hint of thunder or lightning, get off the water immediately and wait until the storm passes by.

Fighting Fish from
a Kayak

ing Fish in a Kayak

Scott plays a big red fish perfectly in the flats of Texas.

Now we've gotten you through the selection of your kayak and gear, you've learned about safety, and you've become an outstanding paddler. We've even touched on some of the methods used to fish from a kayak in different situations. You are starting to walk the walk and talk the talk. So what's next? Like our buddy Dean Thomas always says, "You sure talk like you know what you're doing, but sooner or later you're gonna have to catch a fish." He's right. That's why you got into this whole thing in the first place. You wanted to catch fish from a kayak. We can all say it isn't about catching fish, it's about the exercise or it's about the pure pleasure of getting outdoors. While those things are great and sound cool to talk about, we all really know…it's about the fish.

So a fish finally cooperates and you find yourself at one end of a tug-o-war with a finned adversary. What do you do now?

You would be surprised how many people who have just started kayak fishing fail to plan for this part of the adventure. We've had the front row seats for some pretty funny scenes when the two parties meet for the first time. Rods get broken, people drop their nets in the water, and on one occasion a five-point redfish flipped a 200-pound grown man off his kayak. That fella looked pretty silly sitting in the water in the mud right next to his trusty steed. Luckily it only injured his pride. In deeper water it could have been serious.

The way to avoid this dilemma is by being prepared and having a plan. The biggest part of the plan is having a good idea what type and size of fish you are targeting. It doesn't hurt to know what other non-targeted fish might be encountered in the area. For instance, take fishing in the surf zone just outside the

breakers for speckled trout. These fish generally run from 3 to 5 pounds with an occasionally larger fish, but anything over 10 pounds is extremely rare. You can rig up for this easily enough with standard bay gear. A medium/light action rod and reel, 12-pound line, and a variety of lures will do the trick. To land one of these fish is a simple matter of reaching out and grabbing them with a firm grip across the back or by netting them. There are no problems with this plan except that trout aren't the only possibility out there. What happens when a twenty-pound king mackerel attacks your lure? It isn't normal, but it isn't all that unheard of either. Kings are extremely fast predators with razor sharp teeth. The possibilities for disaster large or small abound in this situation for the unprepared angler.

Big fish are much stronger than you think and are quite capable of inflicting serious injury if improperly handled. This is not meant to discourage anyone from paddling after the biggest meanest fish to ever swim, just don't try it the first time you go out. Get comfortable with your equipment and hone your abilities on smaller species while working your way up to the big leagues. There are people new to kayaking who are dead set on fishing the surf zone and ocean passes for mature redfish. These brutes can easily top forty pounds and they live in an environment that can be downright dangerous even for experienced kayakers. Beginners and even some people with years of experience have no business out there pursuing fish like this. We wrote this chapter to give you a foundation to work from and give you some things to consider before you inevitably become attached to a fish that is bigger than you planned.

FIGHTING FISH FROM A KAYAK

Hooking and fighting a fish is the rush that brings us back time and again. No matter how many fish you've caught, doing it from a kayak is a whole new experience. If you hook a big enough fish, you'll suddenly find yourself being pulled across the water. It is an odd feeling the first few times a fish grabs a hold of your lure and spins your 'yak around like a weather vane. The coolest trip you'll ever have in kayak fishing is when a truly big fish decides to head for the horizon with you in tow.

While targeting smaller pan-fish and such, getting towed around isn't a concern. For this type of fishing, you only need to sit at anchor or with your feet on the bottom in shallow water to hold your position. It doesn't get much easier.

With somewhat larger fish inshore or in lakes it may become necessary to plan for being towed or at the very least spun around. This is fine out in open water on a calm day. Kick back and enjoy the ride. However, if you're in a situation where being towed could be unsafe or cause you to lose the fish due to some line-entangling structure, then you need to do something. In shallow water it is fairly simple to stop yourself if you're in a sit-on-top. Simply swing your legs over the side and plant your feet firmly on the bottom. Problem solved. Another tactic to use in shallow water with a sand or mud bottom is to deploy a stake-out pole that is tethered to your kayak. Once the fish is on, you grab the stake-out pole and stick it into the bottom. You can also place the pole through one of your scupper holes instead of having it tethered like an anchor. This is very quick, simple, and effective.

Deeper water requires a little more forethought. If you are not already at anchor, then you must be prepared to deploy it. This sounds easy enough until you try it while being pulled across the water with your drag screaming. At that moment you'll want to have your anchor handy and ready to go. Now is not the time to retrieve the anchor from your tankwell, clip it to your kayak, and hope the rope isn't tangled.

There is another very quick and effective method for dealing with these situations. Like most good ideas, this one was born

Fishing at anchor.

rod holder. The location of the anchor depends on which hand you crank your reel with. If you use your left hand, place the anchor in a rod holder just behind and to the left of your seat. You can then ease along casting perpendicular to the shoreline trees. Once a fish is hooked, hold the rod with one hand and toss out the anchor with the other. The anchor grabs the bottom and with a tight drag you've got a fighting chance at keeping the fish out of whatever line-cutting structure is around.

The opposite of that situation is when you are fishing at anchor and hook up with a very large fish in open water. It is often advantageous to let a big strong fish tow you around a bit. You are in effect using your kayak as drag to wear the fish down. The problem is that you can't very well retrieve and stow your anchor while doing battle. The solution here is to attach the anchor to your kayak using a quick release clip and have a brightly colored float rigged on the rope near the clip. Once a fish is on the line, release the anchor clip and fight your fish. When the fight is over, locate the float and paddle back to it. Then you can either retrieve the anchor or reattach it to your kayak and resume fishing in the same spot.

from necessity while fishing in Florida for snook way back in the mangroves for the first time. Snook are ambush feeders and they love to hang close to the edges of the trees. Their immediate response to feeling the sting of a hook is to turn and run straight into a tangle of mangrove roots. These fish were simply yanking our kayaks right into the trees. We were getting schooled and the tally of lost lures was mounting. The problem was that the water was too deep to touch bottom and it was necessary to remain mobile while working down the shoreline. Anchoring would have been ineffective.

The solution was to set the anchor up with a length of rope just long enough to hit bottom and with enough scope to allow the anchor to grab. The anchor rope is then clipped on to a cleat or pad eye and the shank of the anchor is placed in a flush-mount

Another twist on using your kayak as drag to tire out a fish is to deploy a drift anchor during the fight. This will produce a serious amount of drag, but also increases the odds that the fish could foul in the trailing line or the drift anchor. We have a friend in Florida who often uses this technique for landing ridiculously large tarpon from his kayak.

Captain Dean Thomas puts pressure on a fish heading to the stern so that he can pivot his kayak and avoid his other fishing rods.

Inevitably a fish will run underneath your kayak. You need to quickly assess the situation and determine whether or not you can turn the fish. Hopefully you'll be able to impose your will and bring it back out from under the boat. Should you realize that this won't work, you'd better be ready to react quickly. The big fellow we mentioned earlier found himself in this position and made the momentary mistake of leaning over the side of the kayak to see where the fish was going. He was out of the kayak and sitting in the mud before he knew what happened. A large fish can easily flip you over or break a rod against the side of the kayak. The best thing to do is extend your rod tip towards the front of the kayak, clear the line around the bow, and resume the fight. This might not work if the fish went under the kayak and angled towards the stern. The best way to handle that situation is to extend the rod tip at an angle out and back towards the stern while bearing down and putting as much pressure as you dare on the fish. The goal here is to pivot the kayak. It probably won't work too well if you have an anchor out.

Something else to practice is using one arm to paddle. It is a very handy skill to have in your arsenal. This usually comes into play in moving water or when a fish is towing the kayak towards an obstacle. Be aware of your surroundings and be prepared to use the paddle to maneuver. I like to position the paddle with the center near my elbow and the shaft along the outside of my forearm. With a firm grip I can now brace the shaft of the paddle against my forearm and reposition the kayak as needed.

The secret to success with any of these methods is in knowing exactly what the plan is before you ever hook the fish. You must be familiar with your equipment and have the ability to use it without having to take your mind off the fight. Battling a big strong fish from a kayak is challenging enough when you've got it all together—imagine what it would be like if you were completely unprepared for the experience.

LANDING FISH IN A KAYAK

As stated previously, catching small fish from a kayak doesn't require much forethought or planning. Quite often it is just a matter of hoisting them into the cockpit while they're still hooked. Large fish are a completely different story, as are toothy critters. Again, knowing your quarry and being prepared

A lip gripping tool, like Boga grips, protect both your hands and the fish.

for the possibility of incidental catches will help. Common sense will determine whether you'll be using your hand, a net, a lip-gripping tool, or possibly a gaff.

For instance, barracuda are a real possibility on the flats in Florida, even though the target is bonefish. There's a huge difference in safely landing these two fish. A bonefish is easily picked up with a hand placed under its belly while a barracuda's vicious teeth and generally bad attitude demand respect and a cautious approach.

A few words about conservation seem appropriate at this point. If you intend to release the fish it is best to use a lip-gripping tool or your hand. Nets are tough on a fish's protective slime coating—and while the fish might appear to be fine when it's released, it could suffer from skin infections later on. A lip-gripping tool is very effective for gaining control of a fish and minimizes the amount of handling required to

unhook and release it. Just remember that the classic fish photo method of hanging a large fish vertically by its lips can cause injury to the jaw hinge and internal organs. If you'd like to get a picture of your catch before releasing it, try holding it horizontally with one hand supporting the belly. Should you choose to use your hand, always wet it prior to grabbing the fish to lessen the effects on its slime coating.

The final moments of fighting a fish are critical to safely landing it. The majority of fish lost happen within a few feet of the angler. There's a combination of factors that conspire to cause this last-second escape. Excitement overtakes reasoning and good judgment. The trophy seems to be a sure thing and the angler prematurely makes a grab causing the fish to surge away. At this point physics takes over. There is less line to act as a shock absorber and the rod is bent to the point that it has also lost its shock-absorbing qualities. Without the extra

By bending the elbow and bringing the reel into the body when the fish is in close, your arm can provide some of the shock-absorbing qualities that your rod and line can no longer deliver.

give in the rod, the pressure on the hook increases and it pulls free or the line breaks. To provide a little insurance, many experienced anglers will back off on the drag just a bit as the fish gets closer. Another thing you'll see great anglers do is to sharply bend at the elbow bringing the reel up close to their body. If the fish makes a sudden surge they can then extend their arms, allowing for a bit of give to the fish. The angler who can remain calm and steady will be the one who consistently lands the trophy fish.

When in shallow water many anglers choose to exit their kayak and bring the fish to hand while standing in the water. This is a great tactic if you are certain of the depth of water and the composition of the bottom. Stepping out into deep water or onto a soft bottom will not win you any style points with your fishing buddies, but the good news is you'll be the center of attention back at fish camp during the story-telling

hour. So if you are the least bit uncertain of either, you're much better off staying put in your boat.

The key to landing large fish whether wading, in a boat, or in a kayak is to play the fish until it is properly tired to the point it is safe to handle. The last thing you want in the kayak is an out-of-control fish. In fact, very large fish that you intend to release are best left in the water alongside the kayak. Keep in mind that maintaining your weight over the center line of the kayak will help you remain upright. Leaning over to hoist a big fish into the cockpit could lead to an unexpected swim. You must realize that the fish's weight does not have any impact on your balance while it is in the water. As you lift that fish from the water the amount of off-center weight increases and you need to compensate by placing an equal amount of your weight towards the opposite side of the kayak. Know the limits of stability on your particular kayak and don't exceed

it. It sounds so simple, but in the heat of the moment the excitement can cause a lapse in judgment.

Do yourself a favor and get as much information as possible about the fish you may encounter, especially in saltwater. Some, like barracuda or king mackerel, have obviously dangerous dentures, while others conceal their defenses. A snook can safely be grabbed by the lower lip in the classic bass-fishing manner. However, they have a razor sharp gill plate that has cut many an unsuspecting angler. Spotted sea trout look innocent enough, but they've got a set of needle sharp teeth towards the front of their mouth that will cause a serious puncture wound should you attempt to grab by the lip.

Know your quarry and you'll be better prepared to deal with the chore of landing.

Should you decide to keep a few fish for dinner, you'll need to find a way to store them. A stringer is simple and generally effective. You can also carry along a soft-sided ice chest or one of the insulated bags designed for bringing your cold foods home from the grocery store. Another option is to get one of the insulated kayak fish bags that are specifically designed to be used by kayakers. These triangular shaped soft-side coolers can be strapped to the front deck or placed in the rear tankwell and will hold a surprising amount of ice and fish.

Fishing Lakes and Ponds

Fishing Flowing Rivers

FRESHWATER
KAYAK FISHING

Kayaks are unrivaled for getting into the little weedy back channels in lakes and ponds.

FISHING LAKES AND PONDS

Some of my fondest memories from growing up as a kid are of fishing on the lakes of Maine for bass and perch out of the family canoe. Back then, canoes were the norm and kayaks were scarce. The industry didn't exist 30 years ago and your choices were limited. Sit-on-tops weren't even invented yet.

Today's modern kayaks, whether sit-on-tops or sit-insides, are a great way to enjoy fishing on your local lake or pond. A lot of the techniques already discussed in this book apply to lake fishing. Paddling strokes, paddling safety, and re-entry techniques are all the same. The biggest hazard I've ever encountered on a lake is inebriated power boaters. Remember, one of the coolest things about kayaks is that they don't draw very much water, giving you access to shallow water that power boaters can only dream about. Stick closer to the edges of the lake whenever possible. The fishing is usually better, there's more to see, and you stand a better chance of avoiding power boaters towing people on inner tubes. With a little knowledge of where you are going, a look at the weather forecast for the day, and some thoughtful preparation, you're all set.

FISHING FLOWING RIVERS

By Joel McBride

"Can I take this boat on the river?" Without more information, this question is impossible to answer. What kind of river are they talking about? I've spent 20 years of my life as an avid whitewater kayaker and have visited rivers of all shapes and sizes all over the globe. Some are suited for kayak fishing and others not. Let's take a look at the differences.

CLASSES OF RIVERS

Moving water presents a new set of challenges and obstacles. Throughout the world, rivers are rated in classes from I to

Flowing rivers provide some of the best fishing and kayaks can get you to spots that are otherwise inaccessible.

It's usually easiest to hop out of your kayak and fish from shore.

VI. Class I is essentially flat water, class VI is un-navigable. Depending on your ability level, I think class I and II are appropriate for kayak fishing, while all others are not.

I live along the banks of the Arkansas River, high up in Colorado. This is a well known fishery for Brown and Rainbow trout and people come from all over the country to float fish it in drift boats or rafts. The best fishing is of course outside the high runoff and the "Ark" is a meandering class II-III river in the prime fishing sections when it's low. Even though I have the paddling skills to easily paddle this river, and have done so a thousand times, it's simply too busy to fish it efficiently from a kayak. You constantly have to pick up your paddle to make adjustments to your course and avoid hitting rocks. For rivers like this, it isn't that you don't have the skills or aren't up to the task. It just won't be a very productive day of fishing for you, so you have to choose your rivers based on what you want to do.

There are many class II to IV rivers that offer less continuous whitewater and that can provide great kayak fishing options, albeit only for experienced whitewater paddlers. These rivers tend to be drop/pool in character, meaning that the rapids are usually caused by water spilling from one lake into another, or more generally that sections of whitewater are followed by sections of flat water. The problem with kayak fishing on these types of rivers is that although you may have the skill to safely and reliably navigate the rapids in a whitewater kayak, by taking a loaded kayak fishing boat through the whitewater, you could easily lose all your gear. If you're interested in kayak fishing on more than class I or light class II whitewater, you will have to bring a lot less equipment because it will all need to be stowed and secured inside the kayak. If you are a whitewater kayaker and know what you're doing, by all means, pack a bit of fishing gear that fits in your boat and go down anything you know you can handle. You will likely do all your fishing from out of your kayak, but you'll have access to pools, eddies and small bays that may have never before seen a lure. For the sake of this book, however, we are going to ignore class III and higher, and just focus on some of the things a typical kayak fisher may encounter on class I and light class II whitewater.

ANATOMY OF A RIVER

The first thing we're going to look at is the anatomy of a flowing river. Simplified, a flowing river has current and eddies. The current is the water moving downstream. Usually there's a main channel but a mid-stream rock or an island can divide the main current and form multiple channels that all have current. An eddy is a pocket of water directly downstream from some form of obstruction, for example, a rock or a part of the river bank that juts out. The deflection of water by the obstruction creates a relatively calm area below—a paddler's parking spot. The concept is quite simple. When water is deflected by an object, it's pushed away from one area and towards another, creating a differential in the amount of water between the two areas. Because of gravity, the river naturally wants to equalize this differential by flattening itself out. To achieve this, the water circles back into the area that it was originally deflected away from. The result is an eddy on the downstream side of the obstruction. This flow creates an upstream current (from bottom to top) in the eddy that can vary in strength from being

Brendan sits comfortably in the calm water of the eddy, just on the outskirts of the main current.

almost unnoticeable (on gentle, slow rivers) to very powerful (on fast-flowing, big volume rivers). An eddy line forms where the upstream-flowing water of the eddy (the eddy current) meets the downstream-flowing water of the river (the main current), creating a helical (whirlpool-like) flow that is usually fairly easily distinguishable as a rough line. The eddy line is narrowest and most crisply defined at the top of the eddy and it dissipates toward the bottom of the eddy.

GETTING TO THE FISH

Now that you understand basic river dynamics, let's look at the practicalities of kayak fishing in flowing rivers before we look at some of the hazards. As any river angler knows, fish love to hang out in eddies and wait for the main current to bring the food to them. Experienced kayakers can use the kayak to get to spots on rivers that are otherwise inaccessible to other anglers. That may simply be the eddy on the other side of a popular fishing river. In many cases, it will be most convenient to hop out of the kayak, pull it up on shore and move along the riverbank. Of course, in order to paddle safely in anything more than class 1 current, you must take a whitewater kayaking course. By doing so, you'll open the doors to vast new fishing territory and you might even find that you enjoy the whitewater paddling aspect as much as you like the fishing!

FROM PUT-IN TO TAKE-OUT

Something else to consider is that if you are going to paddle a river with any moving water, chances are that you are not going to take out your boat at the same spot you put in. You'll need to leave one vehicle at the bottom and take another to the top. It's also a good idea to know how many river miles it is between the put in and the take out. It's never the same as distance you drove to set up the shuttle. Be aware of the flow of the river too. When the river is up, or has more water in it, it'll take you downstream faster; when it's low, the opposite is true. Know your pace so you don't get stuck paddling in the dark.

RIVER HAZARDS AND SAFETY

Moving water, even slow-moving water, is a powerful force. Just as important as being able to read the water to know where to cast, you need to be able to read the water to know what it's doing and where it's going. This is a critical part of identifying hazards so you can avoid them. Paddling and fishing on flowing rivers are two of my favorite activities. With a little common sense and forethought, they can be done very safely.

Strainers

Strainers are probably the most common and dangerous obstacles on any river. A strainer is a pile of logs or other debris that has been stacked up by the current over time, usually against a rock or bridge abutments. They are called strainers because they work just like pouring pasta and hot water into a colander. The pasta is stopped by the colander while the water passes through the holes. With a strainer on the river, a kayak can get pinned like the noodles against the strainer while the water passes through. The difference is that the water never stops flowing on the river, and the longer you and your boat are pinned there, the worse it gets. It can be extremely dangerous to get caught against a strainer—even in what you think is fairly light current—and if you get pulled under, rescue can be near to impossible. If your kayak gets pinned and you can still get yourself out and on to land, it is often wise to consider abandoning your boat and get help later to pull it out. A boat and gear can be replaced—you can't be. Of course, the best thing to do with strainers is to identify them from upstream and give them a wide berth, completely avoiding them from the start.

Low Head Dams

Low head dams are an extremely hazardous obstacle on the river. For starters, they are very difficult to see from upstream until it is too late. Because a low head dam is man made, it is built with a perfectly horizontal pour-over line, causing it to form a perfect hydraulic on the other side. Among fire departments and river rescue circles, low head dams are

Experienced whitewater kayakers Brendan and Joel run through a class II rapid. Notice the thigh straps they use for extra boat control, and that their fishing gear is all safely stored in the kayak.

referred to as "drowning machines". The only plan of attack here is to know whether the river you are paddling that day has one on it or not. If it does, know where it is, take out well above it, and portage to a spot well below it before putting back in. Leave nothing to chance with a low head dam. Have a plan and stick to it.

Foot Entrapment

The foot entrapment is one of the most common causes of death in shallow, moving water. What happens is that when standing up in current, your foot can get lodged between rocks or anything else on the riverbed. With your foot stuck, the current can easily knock you over and even a light current can make it impossible to get up or unstuck. Foot entrapments can easily lead to a drowning in as little as two feet of water. Being a good swimmer is irrelevant. Avoiding a foot entrapment is easy—simply don't wade out into fast moving water. If for some reason you do find yourself swimming in fast-moving current, resist the temptation to stand up and walk to shore, even if you're in only a few feet of water. Swim your way right into shore and out of the main current before you attempt to stand.

Using Anchors

In kayak fishing, anchors are a popular way to keep your boat in one spot. Generally speaking though, anchoring in moving water is a very bad idea. If you must, make sure you do it from either the bow or stern of the boat. When an object is stationary in current, the water tends to "pile up" on the upstream side of that object. Notice how bridge abutments on the upstream side are constructed in a V-shape. This so the water won't pile up and push on the bridge. When you drop your anchor in current and your boat becomes stationary, the water will pile up on it, flip you to the upstream side, and pull your boat underwater—much like a foot entrapment does to a person. If you are going to experiment with anchoring in moving water, make sure you bring along a knife so you can cut the line quickly if you have to.

erstanding Tides and Tidal Currents

Dealing with Surf

ater Fishing Hazards

SALTWATER KAYAK FISHING

chapter seven

UNDERSTANDING TIDES AND TIDAL CURRENTS

If you plan on doing any kayak fishing in saltwater, you need to have an understanding of tides and tidal currents because they can have a profound impact on your paddling and fishing plans. The first thing to understand is that there is a difference between tides and tidal currents. Tides are the vertical movement of water up and down while tidal currents are the horizontal movements of the water. Tides and tidal currents result from the gravitational effects of the moon on the earth's oceans. As such, tides are predictable in both height and strength of current based on the position and phase of the moon as well as the time of year. There are tide tables available for every part of the world that will provide the tide level as well as the amount of flow.

There are a few terms you need to become familiar with in order to begin to understand how tides will affect your fishing. Flood tides are when the water is rising. Ebb tides are when the water is dropping. The high tide is when the water is at its highest and low tide is when the water is at its lowest. Simple enough, but that is just the beginning.

The commonly available tide charts will provide you with information about the height of the water at a given time in a given place. Tides vary greatly throughout the world with some locations having twenty or more feet of difference between the high and low while other places will have less than a foot of change. The tide level can be crucial to choosing an area to fish depending on the species of fish you are seeking. Local knowledge is priceless when it comes to predicting where the fish will be on a given tide.

Although in some areas tides can have a dramatic effect on water levels, tidal currents will usually play a bigger part in locating feeding fish. For any tidal change there is a time of maximum flood when the water is flooding in at its greatest speed, and a time of maximum ebb, when water is flowing back out at its greatest speed. Between the flood and ebb times there are periods when the movement slows or even stops and then resumes, called "slack tide". As an angler, you are looking for the periods when the current first begins moving or just before it stops moving. These are often the times when the bite really turns on. Moving water causes nature's food store to come to life. Slack tide is dead water and there will be very little feeding activity during that time. It is also true that the fishing will sometimes shut down when the current is at its strongest.

On a recent trip to Tampa Bay, the effects of water movement on fish were very clearly illustrated to us. It was dead low tide with no movement. We had parked the kayaks and were walking along an exposed sandbar. Several big fish were visible, lying nearly motionless in the scattered sand potholes of the grass beds. These fish refused every lure that we danced right in front of them. It was tough to sit there looking at these huge redfish and snook, knowing they weren't going to bite. After a while, the standing grass began to waver as the tidal flow slowly started to move. Within minutes those same fish were feeding and consistently taking the very same lures that they had previously snubbed. It was a dramatic and obviously tide-influenced incident.

Something that is often overlooked in all of the tide talk is the wind. Wind-driven currents are sometimes as useful as tidal currents. On our flats in Texas we'll often have less than a foot of difference between the high and low tide. Spread this out over the several hours between the high and low tides and you will understand that there is very little tidal current being produced. In situations like these, seek out the wind currents. The wind pushes the water across the open areas and piles water against the far shoreline. Any islands or breaks in the shoreline will funnel these wind currents and accelerate them to the point that they become useful for locating fish.

The old salts had far less information at their disposal than we do today and were much more in tune with the ways of nature. They almost instinctively understood how the tides worked and what effects they would have on the fishing. Today we have tons of information at our fingertips. Within a few minutes on a computer we can know about the tide, current, water temperature, and the weather conditions—without ever even going near the water. While all of this information is great, you still need to learn how it applies to your area and the fish you seek. There is no way that we could cover every species and every

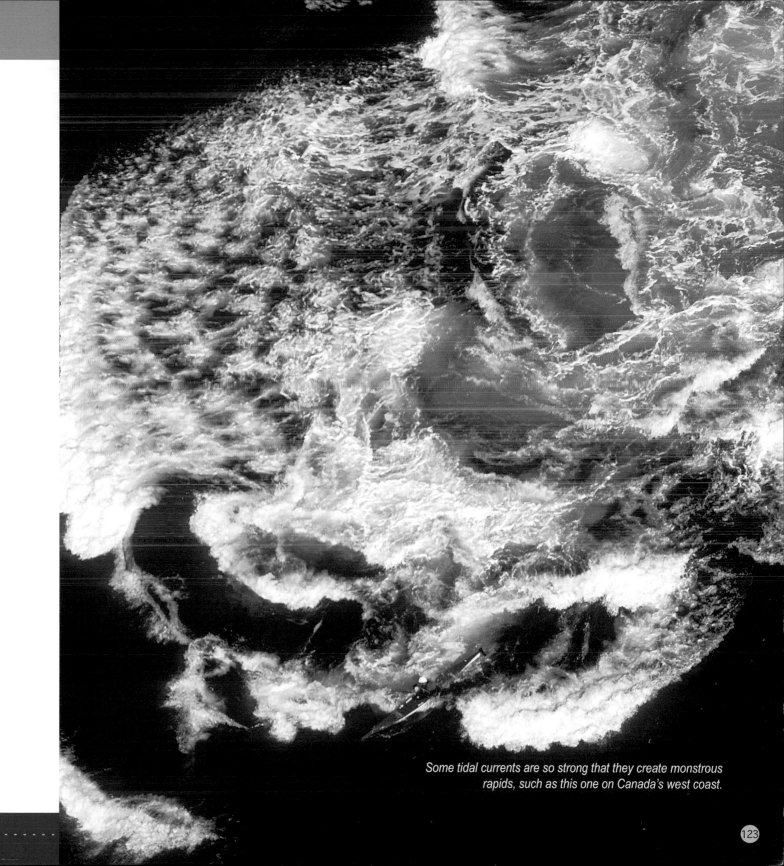

Some tidal currents are so strong that they create monstrous rapids, such as this one on Canada's west coast.

A very slow-moving tidal current carries Joel through the mangroves in the Florida Keys.

situation that you may encounter within the scope of this book. That is your homework assignment. It is a lifelong study that can be as entertaining as the fishing itself.

DEALING WITH SURF

If you want to fish beyond a surf zone, you have to learn how to paddle out through the breakers or paddle in through them to a beach landing. With that said, paddling through surf is challenging and it also has the potential of being dangerous because of hazards like rip currents. So, if you plan on paddling in an area that requires navigating through surf, you'll want to take surf/sea kayaking lessons. Surf kayaking lessons will teach you how to launch, break out through waves and then land again. They'll also let you know how to deal with different rescue situations that could arise.

SALTWATER FISHING HAZARDS AND SAFETY

In the saltwater environment, it seems at times that almost everything out there is trying to get you. From sharks to rip currents to unseen bacteria, it can be somewhat intimidating.

Every outdoors activity has its challenges and inherent dangers. Paddling and fishing in saltwater presents a unique set of problems that you must be aware of and be prepared to deal with. This is not meant to frighten or alarm anyone. The last thing we want to do is discourage anyone from venturing into the bays or oceans. However, going into any situation with a complete knowledge of the possibilities will keep you safer than if you just pretend that those dangers do not exist. Fear of the unknown keeps far too many people from experiencing life. This section is intended to educate you to the possible dangers and hopefully make your trip to the coast safe and enjoyable.

SHARKS

When inlanders talk about fishing at the coast, the issue of sharks usually comes up. Shark bite incidents are extremely rare and usually involve some sort of situation where the shark has confused a person for baitfish. The vast majority of sharks are nothing more than a nuisance to anglers, if they even show themselves at all. Yes, there are localized areas where sharks are a problem, but for the most part there is little to worry about. The highest risk for an encounter exists when you cart around a stringer of fish, which is fairly self-explanatory. To avoid having problems in areas known to have lots of sharks, simply carry a fish bag along and store your catch in there. The second highest risk is in having a shark become interested in the fish struggling at the end of your line. If the "Grey-Fin Express" decides to take your fish at a distance, it's just a disappointing turn of events. Should that same shark decide the time to eat your fish is at the same moment you try to land it, now you've got a problem. An effective way to avoid this situation is to pay attention to what is going on around your kayak as you reach for the fish. A shark will usually circle around its intended prey before it strikes. If you've become entranced by the fish on the end of your line, it could lead to quite a surprise. Stay aware of your surroundings and you'll probably see the shark before it becomes a problem.

STINGRAYS

Probably the second most frequent fear is of stingrays. Rays have a self-defense mechanism built into their tail in the form of a detachable barb. When threatened, rays whip their tail up over their back and plant their barb into whatever is above them. If you step down onto a ray, you'll likely get a nasty wound. There are ray guard boots and shin guards available to help protect you from the barb, but avoiding the encounter is by far the safest. Short of remaining in the kayak and never setting foot on the bottom, the best way to avoid having a ray encounter is to shuffle your feet. A ray will move out of the way to avoid you if he knows you're coming. Many people who have been struck by rays were hit when they stepped backwards to set the hook or while fighting a fish. As bottom feeders, rays

and ice will only make it hurt more. Heat will not eliminate the pain, but it will make it bearable. A thorough cleaning of the wound and a round of antibiotics are necessary because of the nasty bacteria these guys carry around.

OTHER CREATURES

In addition to the "big two" (sharks and rays), there are numerous other creatures to be aware of. Fish can bite, or poke you with a fin and any number of other creatures such as oysters, barnacles and sea urchins can cause a cut or puncture wound. The biggest threat from a wound in saltwater is from bacterial infection. There are some really nasty bacteria out there in the saltwater environment. It is imperative to clean and treat any wound as soon as possible and then keep an eye on it for any signs of an infection. Should an infection or fever arise, immediately seek medical attention. Some of these bacteria are nothing to laugh about and can cause serious health issues.

WEATHER

Creatures are usually the cause of the most angst to those new to saltwater, but weather and water pose the greater threat to the unprepared angler. If you plan to fish in saltwater, you need to appreciate how quickly and powerfully the conditions can change. High winds, waves, thick fog and thunderstorms can develop with very little warning in this environment. Your best defense is to study the weather before hitting the water and then vigilantly observe changing conditions while you are there. Many people get caught up in all of the fun and fail to pay attention to the brooding clouds on the horizon. Remember the handheld VHF radio we talked about earlier? Most of these have a weather band channel that allows you to listen to updated forecasts and weather warnings from the NOAA. It is a good idea to carry the radio and turn it on every now and then to check on the conditions.

are attracted to the disturbed bottom and will often follow you around as you wade. Don't be alarmed. It isn't stalking you, it's just doing its thing. Just don't inadvertently step backwards onto it while it's at the dinner table. If you are unfortunate enough to get struck by a ray, place a hot water compress on the wound and immediately seek medical attention. Do not use ice on the wound! The poison in the barb is protein-based

TIDES AND CURRENTS

Tidal flows and levels can also pose a problem for the unprepared. Currents can abruptly change direction between the ebb and flood. At best this could leave you with a tough paddle back to your launch. At worst it could become life threatening. You don't want to get caught in a channel during a strong outgoing tide. The funneling effect of the constricted channel will accelerate the current leading to a potentially dangerous situation. A paddle craft is no match for the strong tidal flows of ocean passes. During these tide changes the water levels can radically change the terrain that you have to deal with. A low tide can expose reefs and rocks, cause channels to run dry, or reveal mud flats that leave you stranded far from the water's edge. High tides can cover beaches as well as landing and launch sites, and the changing landscape can make you seriously disoriented. The bottom line is that if you're new to an area, ask around to find out about the tide and if there is anything you need to be aware of. Know your tide charts and plan your day accordingly.

Currents off the beach don't necessarily follow the tide charts and are something to be aware of out on the open ocean. Although most people associate current with flowing rivers or channeled areas of the inland waterways, open ocean currents can be quite strong. If you intend to fish off the beach, please study the available charts and predicted currents. Getting pushed away from shore by strong current is a deadly serious ordeal that isn't worth all the fish in the ocean. At beaches, waves can cause strong offshore flows referred to as rip currents. Rip currents are the primary cause of swimmer rescues at surf beaches because they can be tricky to spot, and are surprisingly powerful. These currents form when water that has been pushed up on a beach by breaking waves retreats to the open water. Because waves continually push more water up the slope of the beach, there can be a lot of water searching for the quickest way back out, and strong rip currents can take you a lot farther out than you imagined or planned. Should you ever get caught in a rip current, the way to escape it is to move perpendicular to the current until you're

One key to staying safe is educating yourself about all the possible dangers in an area before you head out.

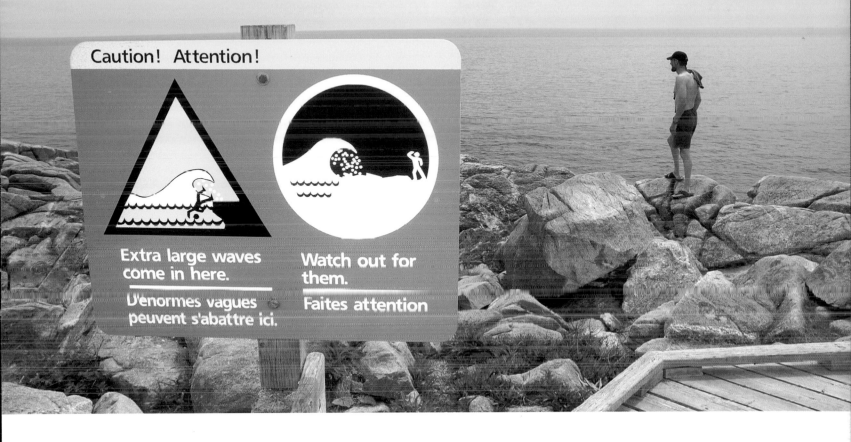

Caution! Attention!

Extra large waves come in here.

D'enormes vagues peuvent s'abattre ici.

Watch out for them.

Faites attention

free. Fortunately, public beaches that are subject to strong rip currents usually have lots of warning signs and are well known by the locals. If you do decide to launch from the beach, keep in mind that for other beach users, you're going to be the biggest hazard! When caught in a wave, your kayak becomes a plastic torpedo and can really hurt other swimmers.

THE OTHER GUY

The final danger is "the other guy". This applies to both fresh and saltwater. You are no match for a powerboat or even a small sailboat. We understand that in most situations you do have the right-of-way because you are in a human-powered vessel, but

that is not what you want chiseled onto your tombstone. "He had the right-of-way." You need to be alert and cautious while in areas frequented by other boaters. Boat wakes and inattentive drivers can ruin your day. You must realize that while sitting in a kayak you are fairly low to the water and can be somewhat difficult to see in some situations. I don't want to give a boater any excuse for not knowing I'm there. Brightly colored kayaks, clothing and paddles will all make you more visible on the water. Some people have begun to place brightly colored "bicycle flags" on their kayaks to increase their visibility. It is also a good idea to keep some type of noise signaling device close by. Some people carry a small air horn that can get attention from a long distance.

GLOSSARY OF TERMS

Assisted rescue – rescue technique performed with the aid of at least one other person in addition to the swimmer

Back band – a padded band of material that provides back support

Bilge pump – a device for pumping water out of a boat

Bow – the front of a boat

Bowline – a cord attached to the front of the boat – useful for towing or tying the boat to a dock

Bulkhead – a waterproof wall that divides the interior of a kayak, creating flotation and storage areas

Bungee cords (also known as shock-cords) – elastic lines on the deck of a kayak – perfect for securing gear within easy reach (water bottles, sunscreen, ball cap, etc.); see also 'Deck lines' and 'Perimeter lines'

Capsize – when a boat overturns so that it goes from being right side up to upside–down

Cargo – the items transported in a boat

Chart (nautical) – marine map referencing water features, including depths, shorelines, scale, aids to navigation (like lights and buoys), and other features essential to marine navigation

Coaming – the lip around the cockpit that allows the attachment of a spray skirt

Cockpit – the sitting area in a kayak

Compass – a magnetic device that indicates magnetic north and the other corresponding points of direction over 360 degrees

Course – the compass direction of travel to a destination

Deck – the top of a kayak

Deck lines – a rope or shock-cord attached to a kayak's deck, used for securing items on deck or to make it easier to grab the boat; see also 'Perimeter lines' and 'Bungee cords'

Drain plug – a stopper, usually mounted in the stern, which can be removed to drain a kayak

Drift fishing – a fishing technique that involves letting wind or current move the kayak over the area to be fished

Dry bag – a waterproof bag with a seal (usually a roll–top closing system) that keeps contents dry

Ebb tide – the outgoing tide and the resulting decrease in water depth; see also 'Flood tide'

Eddy – the quiet water below an obstacle in current, where water flows back in the opposite direction to the main flow

Edging – to tilt your kayak to one side

Emergency bag – a dry bag that carries enough supplies to survive an unplanned night spent in the wilderness

Feather – the twist, offset, or difference in angles between the two blades of a kayak paddle

Float plan – an outline of the route and schedule of a kayak trip

Flood tide – the incoming tide and the resulting increase in water depth; see also 'Ebb tide'

Foot entrapment – when your foot gets stuck in riverbed debris, a serious hazard

Foot pedals – foot supports that slide on a track to accommodate paddlers of different leg lengths; foot pedals also control the rudder, if a kayak has one

Foot wells – molded recesses in the deck of a kayak where you put your feet when sitting in a kayak

GPS (Global Positioning System) – a battery-powered electronic device that very accurately calculates positions and courses based on satellite information

Handles – the carrying toggles found at the bow and stern of a kayak

Hatch – the opening into a cargo compartment in a kayak

Hull – the bottom of a boat

Kayak – a watercraft propelled by a double-bladed paddle

Knot – a measurement of speed – one nautical mile per hour;

see also 'Nautical mile'

Life jacket – see 'PDF'

Mothership – a powerboat that can transport individual kayaks and anglers as a group to and from the fishing destination

Nautical mile – unit of distance used on the sea – approximately 1.87 kilometers or 1.15 'land' miles; see also 'Knot'

Navigation – the art and skill of determining your position, and selecting a safe route to your intended destination

Paddle – used for propelling the boat by drawing their blades through the water; kayak paddles are double-bladed; canoe paddles have only one blade

Paddle leash – tether that attaches a paddle to a kayak

Perimeter lines – cords that run around the edges of the deck on a kayak, making the boat easier to grab; see also 'Deck lines' and 'Bungee cords'

PFD – Personal Flotation Device – worn like a vest to keep you afloat in water

Portage – to carry a kayak or canoe overland

Power face – the concave side of a paddle blade that catches water during a forward stroke

Put-in – the location where a kayak trip begins; see also 'Takeout'

Re-entry – getting back into a kayak from the water

Rescue – a process whereby people at risk are returned to a situation of safety

Ripcord – the cord at the front of the spray skirt or spray deck that you pull to remove the skirt

Rip tide – strong current on a beach, created by waves – potentially very dangerous

Rod holder – device for holding a fishing rod

Roof rack – system of two bars that mount to the roof of a vehicle for transporting kayaks and other loads

Rudder – a foot-controlled steering mechanism mounted at the back of a kayak

Scupper – a hole that goes through a boat allowing water to drain off the deck back into the sea/lake/river

Self rescue – a rescue technique where the swimmer re-enters their kayak without aid from a second party

Side-saddle – a sitting position that can be used for sit-on-tops with both legs hanging off one side of the kayak

SINK – acronym for a sit-inside kayak

Skeg – a blade or fin that drops into the water to help a kayak go straight

SOT – acronym for a sit-on-top kayak

Spray skirt (also called 'spray deck') – nylon or neoprene skirt worn around the waist – attaches to the kayak coaming to keep water out of the boat.

Stern – back of the boat

Strainer – a pile of logs or other debris that is stacked up by current over time, creating a serious hazard for boaters

Takeout – the location where a paddling trip ends; see also 'Put-in'

Tank well – molded recess in a kayak designed to carry a diver's oxygen tank

Thigh hook, or thigh brace – in some sit-inside kayaks, the curved flange that the leg braces against

Thigh straps – an after-market accessory that attaches to a sit-on-top to allow the kayak to be gripped by the paddler's legs

Tidal rip – a strong current created by changes in tide height

Tide and current tables (also collected in a 'tide and current atlas') – the collected calculations for tide and current information (times, heights, speeds); organized based on the calendar year, so a recent version is required for accurate information

Trolling – a fishing technique that involves dragging a lure or bait behind a boat

VHF (Very High Frequency) – radio system commonly used in the marine environment; limited to a line-of-sight direct path between the transmitter and the receiver

Wind wave – waves formed by the effects of wind on the surface of water

FISH ON!

KAYAK FISHING UPS THE CHANCES

At Wilderness Systems, we understand there is more to the experience than just the catch, there's the thrill of the hunt. With the input from our team we have designed the best boats to get the biggest fish. This means our kayaks cover more water, and get closer to the fish than any motor boat dreamed possible. **Fish On!**

TARPON ANGLER FAMILY: 120, 140, 160i

Featuring the
Comfort Seating System

Paddling accessories provided by:

www.harmonygear.com

WILDERNESS
SYSTEMS

www.wildernesssystems.com

photo by: Corey Hendrickson

NEW! AT FishStix paddle

Designed on the Xception SL platform, the new AT FishStix paddle combines durability with performance and stealth for the ultimate angling paddle. The full camo graphics and its smooth entry and release are sure to let you fish the best holes even if they are miles from your launch. Full control grips (ergonomic bentshaft design) gives you ultimate blade control for rough water and alleviates over use injuries for full days of hunting out the big ones. One team member, Captain Scott Null says "AT's ergonomic shaft fits perfectly in your hands and the paddles are as light as a feather, but don't think for a minute that they're delicate. These paddles are plenty tough enough to stand up to the every day rigors of fishing in the fresh and saltwater environment."

Try one and you will never go back.

ADVENTURE TECHNOLOGY

www.atpaddles.com

PERCEPTION IS SHAPING THE FUTURE OF KAYAKS.

perception

The Prodigy family of kayaks encapsulates everything that a paddler searches for and more in a recreational kayak. Under the lead of legendary designer Bob McDonough, we've engineered a boat that is ideal for many types of water...lakes, ponds, sounds and slow, deep rivers. Featuring a new high performance v-shape hull with soft chines, the new Prodigy provides a platform that is stable and effortless to paddle and cast, while the new Zone outfitting provides superior comfort and customization. Novices and experts will all agree that with boats like the new Prodigy, **Perception is shaping the future of kayaks.**

☐ BOAT: PRODIGY

☐ HULL: SHALLOW V

☐ LENGTH: 10', 10' EXP and 12'

☐ DESIGNER: BOB McDONOUGH

MTI ADVENTUREWEAR

ANGLER SERIES

MTI offers four models of PFDs tailored to the specific needs of paddling fisher folk. Each is like a cross between a Coast Guard approved personal flotation device and a well designed fishing vest. Lots of pockets to hold everything you will need to take to the water, plus pin-on retractors, lash tabs, D-rings and more, with a choice of colors: classic Olive and Green, Khaki, or a high visibility Red. For more information go to www.mtiadventurewear.com.

CALCUTTA

DORADO

FISHER PRO

FISHER

www.**mti**adventure**wear**.com
1 800 783 4684